A TUDOR STORY

A TUDOR STORY

The return of Anne Boleyn

by

CANON W. S. PAKENHAM-WALSH, M.A.

Published for the Churches Fellowship for Psychical and Spiritual Studies by

JAMES CLARKE AND CO. LTD.
33, STORE STREET, LONDON, W.C.1

First published 1963

Printed by A. Wheaton & Co., Ltd., Exeter, England

CONTENTS

INTRODUCTION

Here at last is the long awaited *Tudor Story*, by the late Canon William Pakenham-Walsh, the third volume in our Churches' Fellowship series of publications. It is a remarkable document, and one which readers may find somewhat diffuse and over-spacious, but which in the main it has been quite impossible to shorten or abridge without damaging the feeling of the story, and obscuring something of the character of the writer, whose integrity, enthusiasm, simplicity (sancta simplicitas) romanticism and essential goodness, courtesy and holiness shine through every page.

Those of us who have been privileged to know him would all subscribe to the verdict passed by a Greater One than ourselves on Nathaniel 'Truly an Israelite in whom there is no guile', as being abundantly true of his character as a disciple of the Lord Jesus Christ.

I say this because this volume can quite obviously be shot down by critics in many places. The Canon, in his earlier contacts with sensitives especially, broke almost every rule of a good 'sitter' – he gave away names and places, and dates even; he suggested answers to which the sensitive usually answered 'Yes', (not unnaturally the critical would say!) and by overhasty identification of signs or symbols often appears to have begged the very case which he thought he was genuinely trying to elucidate or prove. But no one who knew him would ever attribute to him anything other than the most complete integrity (some might call it naiveté) and if this story is not what it appears to be prima facie, then our verdict can only be that the Canon deceived no one but himself. It is clear that he believed implicitly in the objective reality of the story which unfolded itself over so many years and through so many different channels to him.

Yet when all is reckoned up – there are certain elements in this tale which do appear to have intruded spontaneously into the jig-saw pattern – the apparently inexplicable writing of the Lament of Anny Boleyn by Mrs Monson *before* she had ever heard of him or his Tudor interests; as well as the quite mis-understood message regarding 'SEND' which it took the Canon 12 months to unravel, and above the quite extraordinary chain of 'coincidences' – whatever may be the metaphysical explana-tion of these – which led him on from step to step in his knightly pilgrimage as *champion* of this obviously highly wronged and maligned lady of a bygone age. Those who have made even a little progress in the path of spiritual understanding and believe that they have perceived some slight glimmering as to the ways in which Providence works, will perhaps be more impressed with this coincidental framework to the story than those who view it coldly and objectively, because they know how true are New-man's words about 'one step enough for me', which was certainly the Canon's way of approach to his subject, as he sought the guidance of his Master.

There are, it seems to me, only two possible verdicts on this story – one that it is basically and objectively true, and that the picture of the interweaving of the two worlds, and the whole exquisite story of the wise, wonderful, stern and yet infinitely just and loving workings of Our Heavenly Father, of Our Lord Jesus Christ, and of His Holy Spirit accomplishing in human souls 'the purpose of His perfect will' for the forgiveness and ultimate redemption of even the worst of sinners is both ob-jectively and spiritually true: *or* that this *Tudor Story* is the extremely complicated and laboriously worked out projection through the minds of many sensitives and situations of the Crea-tive subconscious inspiration of the Canon himself, writing through many hands, as it were, another and more powerful imaginative drama around the person of the Lady Anne towards whom he had conceived a truly touching and romantic attach-ment and devotion.

Mrs Gwen Vivian, his very old friend to whom we are deeply indebted for the revision and editing of this story, herself a con-vinced believer in the possibility of communication, and inciden-tally in the veracity of this story, has written a book entitled *Love*

Conquers Death. If the first requisite of good communication
with the world of the spirit is the nexus of a genuine, sincere and
selfless love – a factor which can hardly enter into scientific
laboratory experiments and statistical reckonings or evaluations
of E.S.P. – then we can both understand how it is that genuine
contact with the unseen world is so rare, and if genuine often
so banal, because such high love and devotion is so rare a quality
in our workaday world, and also how difficult it is to *prove*
that such contacts are genuine. For the 'sancta simplicitas' of
such a selfless love does not take account of the 'nicely calculated
less or more' of the scientific laboratory, and lays itself open to
many of the slings and arrows of outraged critics against which
it can only cry with Pascal 'Le coeur a ses raisons que la raison
ne connait pas'. (The heart has its reasons which reason cannot understand), or rise up with Browning and answer 'I have
felt'.

It is because the 'feeling' of this story to me is right, that I
venture in spite of much critical raising of mine own eyebrows
at the Canon's lapses in scientific technique, to come down on
the side of the authenticity of this story, on the evidence at
present before me. If God is what I believe Him to be, the God
and Father of our Lord Jesus Christ, a perfectly just, infinitely
patiently and wholly loving Father, and not the ogre of vindictive sadism, or the stern retributive judge more concerned for
the satisfaction of His outraged majesty than with the achieve-
ment of redemptive love, which some theologians have pictured
Him to be, then the process of the redemption of Henry, as well
as the far less important but none the less just vindication of Anne
herself seems to me to be just what ought to happen, and gives
us a profound standard by which to evaluate the lives of many
prominent men and women of history, *sub specie eternitatis*,
giving much food for thought to historian and moralist alike.

I can only hope in faith and trust that God *is* like this. To
me such divine justice tempered by love and mercy gives rise to
feelings of profound penitence, humility, hope and Love. And
if the mechanics of the writings are vulnerable, and could be
completely shot down, and the story shown to be merely the
product of the late Canon's own creative and imaginative inspiration – then it is still of profound significance as an esay in

the moral theology of judgement, and as being the poetic vision
of a noble and saintly man as to the ways in which God's prov-
idential ordering of the universe of spirits is at work. As such it
might be considered a Protestant prose poem of such delicacy of
spiritual vision and such profundity of moral insight as would
make it worthy to be set alongside of the great Roman Catholic
Newman's *Dream of Gerontius,* enshrining perhaps even more
rational moral and spiritual values than the great Cardinal's
poem of life, death, judgement and redemption.

Canon Pakenham-Walsh died in 1960 at the age of 92. He
had prepared the MSS. for publication before his death and we
have felt it wise to leave certain passages relating to this as he
wrote them, because they are also a part of his character.
Whether or not the communications received since his death are
genuine or not (see Appendix) those of us who are Christians will
feel certain that both these great figures of Catholic sympathies
who when on earth knew in part, now know in entirety and see
face to face, and each can say,

> 'And with the morn those angel faces shine
> Which I have loved long since and lost a while'.

JOHN D. PEARCE-HIGGINS.

Putney Vicarage, 1963.

PREFACE

My interest in Queen Anne Boleyn was first aroused in 1917 when I was a missionary in China, 1897–1920 and when I was also acting as Chaplain to the British community in Foochow, in whose excellent library I found Hepworth Dixon's *History of Two Queens* as well as books by Miss Benger (1821), Agnes Strickland, Philip Sergeant, Francis Hackett and others from which I have compiled a brief summary of her life.

W.S.P-W.

QUEEN ANNE BOLEYN

1533–1536

Anne Boleyn was the youngest daughter of Sir Thomas and Lady Boleyn and was born at Hever Castle, Kent in 1507. She had an older sister Mary and a brother George to whom she was greatly devoted and who was executed with her in 1536 and whose body was buried beside her before the altar in the church of St Peter ad Vincula in the Tower of London. There were several other members of the family, whose names, however, do not come into history.

Anne had a governess Simonette and she must have had some knowledge of French when she went to France in 1514–15 as Maid of Honour to Mary Tudor aged sixteen, youngest sister of Henry VIII, and she was present at her marriage to Charles XII of France aged fifty-three, who died a year later, Anne became a great favourite at the French court and returned to England in 1521, when she was about fifteen.

She then became Maid of Honour to Queen Catherine and was betrothed to Henry Percy, son of the fifth Earl of Northumberland and she might have been happily married had she not attracted the notice of the King, who wished her to become his mistress as her sister Mary had been, and on her indignant refusal, he determined to marry her and make her Queen, and in order to do so he ordered Cardinal Wolsey to break off her engagement with Lord Percy, for which she never forgave the Cardinal.

The King then married her secretly and she was crowned Queen on 1st June, 1533 and her daughter Elizabeth was born on 7th September, 1533.

Henry had set his heart on having a son, and the birth of a daughter was to him a great disappointment and estranged her from him, and when in January 1536, the Queen gave birth to a still born son, caused it is generally believed by the shock of coming across Jane Seymour closeted with the King, Anne's doom was sealed and it only remained to find sufficient charges on which to condemn her.

She was committed to the Tower on 2nd May, 1536 and was brought before a selected court of twenty-six 'Earls Triers' on May 10th, among whom her Uncle Norfolk had the cruelty to include her former lover Lord Percy. To his honour, be it recorded, that when he realised that she was about to be sentenced, he rose up from his place and took no part in her condemnation and he died the following year, it is said of a broken heart.

The indictments against the Queen were so preposterous, including even a charge that she had attempted to poison the King, that only one man, the musician Smeaton, under torture, was found capable of accusing her; the others, like Sir Henry Norris, all said that they would sooner die than bring a false charge against an innocent woman.

But the sentence was a foregone conclusion and she was condemned to be burned alive or beheaded according to the King's pleasure.

She was led back to her room in the Tower and Lord Bacon the historian records that 'having protested her innocence with undaunted greatness of mind', she sent the following message to the King:—

> Commend me to His Majesty and tell him that he has ever been constant in his career of advancing me. From a private gentlewoman he has made me a Marchioness, from a Marchioness a Queen, and now that he hath left no higher degree of honour, he gives my innocence the crown of martyrdom.

What probably incensed her uncle Norfolk against her, who was also her judge, was that she had shown marked sympathy with the reforming party in England. She kept in her possession a copy of Tindale's translation of the New Testament and there is in existence a letter signed Anne the Queen giving protection to a merchant who was involved in trouble for importing from Holland some of these precious copies of the Bible. She had also rescued Hugh Latimer from the duress to which Stokeley, Bishop

of London, had committed him and she had appointed him one
of her court chaplains and afterwards Bishop of Worcester.

On Friday, May 19th, the last sad morning of her life, she
rose two hours after midnight and renewed her devotions and
when she was about to receive the sacrament, she sent for Sir
Wm Kingston, the Governor of the Tower, so that he might be
present, when, with the sacred symbols in her hands, she made
her last solemn protestation of her innocence. 'It is difficult' as
Agnes Strickland says, 'to imagine any person wantonly provok-
ing the wrath of God by incurring the crime of perjury at such a
moment for she had evidently no hope of prolonging her life.'

Her great friend Mary Wyatt accompanied her to the scaffold
where she said, 'Good Christian people, I am come hither to die
according to law, for by the law I am judged to die and therefore I will speak nothing against it. I am come here to accuse no
man. I come here only to die and thus to yield myself humbly
to the will of my lord the King. I pray God to save the King.
If any person will meddle with my cause I require them to judge
the best. Thus I take my leave of the world and I heartily desire
you all to pray for me'.

She then with her own hands removed her coif and collar and
gave them to Mary Wyatt and the little book of devotions she
had been using, and with the words 'Lord Jesus receive my spirit'
on her lips, the blow fell and she passed out of her earthly troubles
into the unseen life and the very next day the King married
Jane Seymour.

All modern writers believe that she was innocent, and Philip
Sergeant in his book *The Life of Anne Boleyn,* expresses what
others feel when he writes of the Queen and of those who died
with her:—

It is beyond doubt that they died for no crime at all, and if
the innocence of both sister and brother was not proved by the
way they met their accusers and their death, then it is impossible by gracious courage ever to prove innocence.

In the cruel, immoral, avaricious, treacherous, and lying age
of the Tudors, Anne Boleyn crosses the scene a brilliant, per-
plexing and pathetic figure and vanishes into the darkness, still
only in her youthful womanhood. History – considered in the
light of a record of personages, not of people – would be far
more intriguing were there more in it such as Anne the Queen.

She was not a perfect woman, but who ever was perfect, and when one remembers that her own young love's dream was cruelly shattered and that she was forced by the King into a most difficult position and surrounded by enemies, few Queens would have done so well, and as Sergeant says 'that whatever her faults she was brave, true to her friends, lavish with her gifts where love and charity led her, sincere in her religious opinions and withal a woman of genuine intellectual power'.

Having come to know so much about the Lady Anne from books, and feeling such a great pity for her misfortunes I was anxious, if possible, on my return to England to visit all the places which were closely connected with her life and I have set down some of the main facts connected with her, so that readers of the story which follows may have some slight knowledge of a Queen who has been much misunderstood and because of the many requests which have come to me asking that I should allow some of the experiences related in the story to be given a wider public. I have hitherto refused to permit their publication because I did not consider that the right time had come, but with the great growth of psychic interest and knowledge and especially after the formation of the 'Churches' Fellowship for Psychical Study', I felt that I should put aside my own dislike of publicity and allow the publication of a story which, though it may lead to controversy, should be welcomed by all sincere and earnest seekers after truth.

The experiences related came to me quite unsought and un-expectedly and in some instances ran counter to my own in-herited beliefs, and not being psychic myself I was simply the recorder of what those with psychic gifts told me that they saw or heard. Some half dozen sensitives, all of them Christian women, were drawn into the story, which ran over about a dozen years 1921–1933 intermittently. I did not know any of them before the story began nor did they know one another, nor did they know anything about me or my historic interests, and there was no possibility of collusion between them, nor had they any idea that they were taking part in a long complicated historical drama with a great religious purpose behind it, and they gave their psychic gifts freely, unsought and without any material reward.

I cannot personally see how it would have been possible to compose or invent such a story without some directing mind behind it, nor do I see how an evil mind could succeed in bringing such good out of so much evil.

It is of course possible to put the whole story down to my own vivid imagination, but I know perfectly well that I do not possess such powers, and I shrink even now from the publicity in which the recording of such a story may involve me. The scenes recorded were always opened with prayer either by myself or by the sensitives and came as great a surprise to them as they did to me, and I can see no other explanation for them than that there was directing purpose behind the story in which I, all unworthy, was called upon to play a small and unexpected part.

Therefore I feel that the whole subject should be approached in the spirit inculcated by St Paul when writing to the early Christians in Philippi, he says:—

> My prayer is that your love may be accompanied by clear knowledge and keen perception, testing things that differ, so that you may be men of transparent character and may be blameless in preparation for the day of Christ.
>
> (Phil. I. 9. iv.)
> *Weymouth's translation*

CHAPTER ONE

COINCIDENCES

*'And the man, wondering at her, held his peace, to wit
whether the Lord had made his journey prosperous or
not.'*

GEN. XXIV. 21.

I came home on furlough in November 1919 and one of the first
things I did was to visit the Tower of London. I stood bare-
headed on the Tower Green beside the spot where the Queen
suffered or rather was released from her sufferings, and then I
entered the chapel of St Peter ad Vincula close by, where her
body is interred.

I knew where to look for her grave beside that of her beloved brother George, Lord Rochford, in front of the altar at
the north end. I asked the Yeoman Warder would he kindly
leave me for a few minutes as I wished to be alone, and then I
fulfilled a long looked-for desire by kneeling beside a spot which
had become so sacred to me. And my prayer was simply this,
that if it were possible, and quite in the line of God's will for us
both, that she might be to me a guardian angel.

Not long after this a number of the most remarkable coincidences began to take place, which I shall now relate in their
order. The first occurred in connection with a visit which I paid
to Maidstone in the spring of 1920 to take part in the annual
C.M.S. Missionary festival. As I had no meeting on the Monday
until three o'clock I determined to take the opportunity to visit
Hever, which is about twenty-three miles distant. I had to cycle
most of the way there and back and I realised that my actual
time at Hever would be very short. It was the 3rd May, the
month of her triumph and also of her death, and as I drew near
to the village, I wondered whether it really could now be of any

I

interest to the Lady Anne that someone with such sympathy for
her was approaching her old home and looking eagerly for
glimpses of it between the trees. I passed the Castle gates, crossed
the village green and thinking that the most hopeful plan for
using my little time well was to find the vicar and ask him to
assist me, I dismounted and knocked at the door of the cottage
nearest to the Church.

A girl came out and I asked her could she tell me where the
vicarage was. She said that it was some distance down the road,
but asked me if I wanted to see the Vicar. I told her that I very
specially wanted to see him. 'Well,' she said, 'the Vicar is inside
with my father.'

In a moment the Vicar himself appeared and then I told him
my errand. He said that I was very fortunate to find him as he
was only just over for a sick call and in another few minutes
would have been at the far end of the parish.

He then got the Church keys and very kindly took me over the
building, showing me the well-preserved tomb of Sir Thomas
Boleyn with its fine Tudor brass above it. The old pews have
gone, but otherwise the Church remains the same as it was when
she worshipped there with her sister Mary and her brother
George, and doubtless at times the faithful Mary Wyatt and her
father Sir Thomas, and of course the old French governess
Simonette, not to speak of the more important Tudor personages who must often have been there, Cramer and Norfolk and
the King himself.

Who could stand in such a spot and be unmoved? I asked the
Vicar if I could see over the castle, but he said that the castle
was not open to the public.

My twenty-three mile ride back to Maidstone was a very
happy one because fortune had smiled upon me and I had been
able to use my precious half hour so well.

About a fortnight later I went to preach in St Mary's Church,
Southampton, I was the guest of the Vicar, Mr Lovell (later
Bishop of Salisbury). I had somewhere heard that a Miss Lovell
had written a play on the Lady Anne and I very much wished
to see it, but on receiving the invitation I did not even remember the fact, and had no idea where Miss Lovell lived. The
moment, however, when I saw Mrs Lovell it suddenly came to

me that she might be the mother of the Miss Lovell who had written the play. It seemed almost impossible that I should be so fortunate, but later in the evening I discovered that it really was so. It was the eldest daughter of my hostess who had written the play, and though she herself was from home, her mother showed me the manuscript.

The writer had evidently no intention of publishing her work, but the idea then first occurred to me that the story would lend itself to a historic drama.

When I had developed the idea, I wrote to Miss Lovell and informed her of my intention to defend the Lady Anne in a play, but that I was approaching the subject from a completely different stand-point to hers. She very kindly wrote back wishing me well in what she evidently considered a very difficult undertaking, adding with a touch of womanly sympathy for her far off sister, 'I am sure poor Anne must be grateful to you for her defence.'

Here then was the second strange coincidence, that I should be invited to the very one house in England where this play had been written and where I should get the idea of telling the story of the Lady Anne in a drama, for I had not up to that time ever thought of making my gathered information public.

I had completed the first act of my play in the August of 1920 and then we all met as a clan in an old vicarage at Eastbourne, which we had taken for the month of September.

We were over twenty in number and the great event of the gathering was to be the silver wedding of my eldest brother, just home from India, and in order to celebrate the occasion the first act was to be performed privately by members of the family, while I was to act as stage-manager.

I cycled down from Farnham, about seventy miles, reaching Eastbourne in the evening. Entering the vicarage, I was passing through the rather dark hall when my attention was arrested by a picture high up near the ceiling and hardly visible in the evening light. I stood for a moment and then I was certain of it, it was a picture of the Lady Anne Boleyn. The clan was incredulous, so a ladder was procured and the question was soon settled by finding her name upon it. It proved to be a very old picture, painted on wood, and most probably from life. It resembled her portrait in the National Portrait Gallery, London, but it was a younger face, painted probably in the old happy days at Hever and before she became Queen.

And so it came to pass that the Play was first performed under, as it were, the gaze of the heroine herself, and I ask is there another house in England, where such a coincidence would have been possible? On returning from Eastbourne I set to work in earnest to finish the play, and to my surprise I found myself awakening each morning at about half-past three with a great desire to get up and write. I obeyed this inclination, and so the tragedy was written in the early mornings between three and six o'clock, when the house was absolutely quiet and I could not be disturbed. Then the scenes presented themselves vividly and the flow of the thought came quickly, it was just my part to feel as it were for the words in which to endeavour to express the impressions.

I finished my play in the October of 1920. Very soon after I received a letter from my sister asking had I seen the accounts published in the English illustrated papers of a film made in Berlin, at enormous cost, about the Lady Anne Boleyn. It appears that the film abounded in serious historical errors and misrepresentations, and I felt that I had been moved to write my play just at a time when it was important that the real story of the Lady Anne should be known.

Some time later I also learned that a cypher of Sir Francis Bacon had been discovered in which he too had written a vindication of the Queen in the form of a play. Although the two plays were separated by three hundred years I was glad to find that my representation agreed in all its main historical features with that of Sir Francis.

There remain two further coincidences which I feel to be significant. I had heard that somewhere in the British Museum there was a Bible which Henry VIII had given the Queen. As I did not know where it was I felt that to look for it without assistance would be a hopeless task. But my studies in the Tudor period constantly led me to the reading room, and one evening as I was hurrying home down the centre aisle of a long room, some Chinese characters to the left caught my eye. I turned aside to look at them; on returning to the central aisle I paused for a moment to look into one of the many glass covered book cases. And there under my eyes was the very Bible I had wanted so much to see! A beautifully bound book with the initials A and H stamped upon it, separated by a Tudor rose.

I had another remarkable experience at Taunton where I had gone to speak at the C.M.S. Jubilee celebrations. As I had a morning free I went pottering about the old Town and came upon a second-hand book shop. A whole quantity of rubbishy books were lying pell-mell in a big box at the entrance, marked one shilling each. I picked one up and to my surprise the title was, *The Anne-Queen Chronicle*. I was almost tossing it back as I thought it must refer to Queen Anne, the sister of Mary II, when I noticed stamped on the green cover the initials A.B. and H.R. Could it possibly be a book about the Lady Anne Boleyn which I had never even heard of? I opened it and read, 'A history of the last five months, faithfully recounted, in the life of the Lady Anne, Marquis of Pembroke, Queen-Consort of England'.

I paid the shilling and took the book home to find in it probably the most full and minute account of the close of the sad tragedy which exists, and it amazes me still that I missed hearing of this book while I was searching for every available source of information and that I came across it in such an extraordinary way unsought, in a second-hand book shop.

If one single coincidence made Abraham's servant wonder whether it was a mere accident or whether his prayer had been granted (see Gen. xxiv), it was but natural that this long series of more remarkable coincidences should raise the same question in my own mind.

CHAPTER TWO

INVITATIONS

'All skirts extended of thy mantle hold
When angel hands from Heaven are scattering gold.'

TRENCH.

HEVER CASTLE

There are three castles in England which are very specially associated with the Lady Anne Boleyn. The first is Hever where she was a girl; the second is Windsor where she was a Queen, and the third is the Tower of London where she was a prisoner.

None of these places is open to the public, for although parts of the Tower and of Windsor are accessible, still permission is not given to see her private royal apartments at Windsor nor 'the little chamber in the Lieutenant's Lodgings', where she spent her last night on earth.

How then could I, an unknown missionary from China gain admission. The days have long gone by when a bold knight errant could blow a bugle outside the walls, and as the defender of a fair lady who had once lived within them, demand an entrance.

But the days of romance are not yet over, and within the short space of one and the same year, the gates of all three castles were flung open and I was welcomed into those portals in the name of the Lady Anne Boleyn herself.

Hever was the first to open. I was speaking in Plymouth and was the guest of an old naval chaplain whom I had known at Hong Kong. I was telling him about the play and my good fortune at Hever in meeting the vicar, but I also spoke of my disappointment in not being able to see over the castle, where the heroine of my play had lived.

He surprised me by saying quietly: 'I am quite sure that if Lady Astor knew of the play and of your great interest in the

6

Lady Anne Boleyn, she would be the first woman in the world to help you in any way she could. She is our member for Plymouth and I shall write at once and ask her.'

He did so, and the result was a very kind letter from Lady Astor expressing her interest in hearing of the play, and extending to me an invitation to visit the castle.

Never will the writer of that letter know all the pleasure which it gave me or the wonder of that afternoon which I spent in the old home of the Boleyn family, nor must I tell of all that I saw there of such intense interest to me, but there is one very remarkable incident in connection with my visit which I may make public.

It was the 27th of January, 1921, but more like a spring day than the middle of winter. I cycled from Farnham along 'the Pilgrim's Way', trained from Guildford to Edenbridge, and then again cycled the last four miles to Hever.

Now, though I had been there before, for some extraordinary reason I cycled right past the great castle gates to a white low wooden gate which I got into my head was the entrance to the drive. How I could make such a mistake I cannot imagine. On reaching this white gate I dismounted, took off my cap and walked. I had not intended to do this, but it seemed the only right thing to do when entering the demesnes of the Lady Anne Boleyn.

As I advanced, the drive narrowed and to my surprise I saw no signs of the castle. I pushed on and after a little while the drive changed into a lane, turned sharp to the left and dived through a tunnel under an embankment. I knew then that I was all at sea, but I went through the tunnel and found myself in a yard where a gardener was potting plants.

We both seemed equally astonished to see each other, and when I told him that I was endeavouring to find Hever Castle, he seemed to doubt my truthfulness and asked me why I had not come in by the main entrance. I said that I had missed it in some way, which must have sounded still more remarkable, since the gateway is a small castle in itself. However, when I showed him Lady Astor's letter of invitation, he gave me the benefit of the doubt, and opening a small door in the wall he ushered me into the lovely gardens, the gardens where my play opens. He shut the gate and there I was all alone in fairyland. There were the two gardeners discussing the return of the Lady Anne from France, then entered Simonette thanking the old gardener for all his pains, and then from the old castle in the distance came the Lady Anne herself.

Time simply faded out that afternoon and I was away back in those Tudor days. I doubtless stood on the very spot where Lord Percy wooed her and where a few hours later the King himself knelt only to be repulsed by her.

But I must not here begin to fill that garden with events and people, though it was full of both that day to me, or I should never get on to what I am trying to say.

After a never-to-be-forgotten hour, I thought I would once again visit the old church just outside the main gates. I approached them this time from the inside, knocked and rang at the towers both to the left and to the right, but there was no response, there was no one on guard and the great gates were locked.

Then I realised how fortunate it was for me that I had made my mistake of an hour earlier, for had I tried to enter from the outside I should equally have failed, nor would I then have dared to venture in by a back way, as I did in all simplicity when I thought I really was on the proper drive. And the result undoubtedly must have been that after knocking for some time in vain, I should have been obliged to return sadly home and bitterly disappointed.

From all this I was saved by making what was a most extraordinary and unaccountable mistake. On my first visit I did not doubt that those great castellated towers were the main entrance, but on this second visit, I somehow got an idea that they led to the stables! What put such an absurd notion into my mind I could not explain, but whatever it was, it proved my salvation that afternoon.

Before I pass on from that most lovely spot in the Weald of Kent and from what was indeed to me the end of a perfect day, I must speak of a very strange thought which seemed impressing itself upon me all through my journey and especially at the Castle itself.

It met me in my morning reading, it rang in my head as I

rode along the country lanes, and at last at Hever it seemed almost blazoned across the old Tudor buildings, and will be for ever associated in my mind with the home of the Lady Anne Boleyn.

I cannot account for it, but I seemed almost to hear these words, 'Our citizenship is in the Heavens'.

It seemed as though someone wanted to write this message not only upon the walls and across the clouds but on my very heart. Yes, I got the impression that the Lady Anne herself was trying to lift me up from dwelling too much upon her old home and the vanished, bygone years, and to remind me that there was something still more wonderful and inspiring to think of than that dear old spot, that her interest and her heart was not now centred in Hever, but that we were both, though separated for the moment by time and space, fellow citizens of a better country, and that my chiefest aim, if I would indeed ever meet her, must be to try to be made meet to be a partaker of the saints in light.

It was with this thought uppermost that I left Hever that evening in the golden sunset, and turned my glittering cycle slowly home.

THE TOWER

My invitation to see 'the little room of sad memories' in the Tower of London, I owe to the kindness of the Resident-Governor and to the good offices of Mr Walter G. Bell, who was so well known for his historical articles in the *Daily Telegraph*. In one of these articles he had thus described that little room:

> Fourteen feet it measures on every side, and there is dark-brown wainscotting of plain oak up to the low ceiling. The White ceiling can almost be touched by an outstretched hand; it is but eight feet above the floor. This was the Queen's room. A spell was upon the place. I thought it the most pathetic prison within the Tower . . . . a little room of sad memories. Instinctively one lowers one's voice when speaking of it.

When I read this account in the *Daily Telegraph*, I took my courage in my two hands and wrote to Mr Bell, telling him of the play and of my great desire to see the last dwelling place of the heroine on earth.

Through his influence, very generously exercised, I received an invitation from the Resident-Governor asking me to join a party of his friends, if possible, on the following Monday at eleven o'clock.

Now it so happened that during that particular week-end, I was preaching near London at Redhill, and so was able to accept, but the Sunday previous I had been in Devonshire and the Sunday following I was away North in Cheshire, indeed, I was not preaching again near London for six months, so the Governor of the Tower, although quite unconscious of the fact, chose the only Monday which was open to me, and thus fortune smiled once more upon me and I was able to present myself at 'the Lieutenant's Lodgings' at the hour appointed.

As I have already given Mr Bell's description of the Queen's prison chamber, I need not repeat it, except to add what he himself also mentions, that over the stone fireplace can still be read the faintly scratched name ANNE.

I shall just give one more extract from Mr Bell's article and then leave that little sad room in reverent silence.

> In this little room one must believe, in such privacy as was allowed to her in her bed-chamber, Anne Boleyn wrote the famous and touching letter to King Henry VIII. (It is given in full at the end of the Play.)
>
> Here, if tradition does not belie, Anne Boleyn woke early in the dark of a May morning to hear Mass and prepare for the end, so these four walls were the last she looked upon before she went down the stairs and out to the scaffold.

WINDSOR

To see the royal apartments of the Lady Anne at Windsor seemed to me an impossibility. I knew of no one who could help and I was not even sure that the rooms were still in existence.

But Windsor too opened its gates, and that in a remarkable way. A military knight, Sir Montague Brown, who had lodgings within the castle, became interested in the play in a roundabout way, and of his own accord sent me an invitation to visit him.

But little did I guess what he had in store for me when my wife Maud and I accepted his kind invitation. We were met at the door by a maid who led us up a spiral stone staircase. At the head of the stairs stood the knight, a fine old general over eighty years of age. After introducing us to his wife he quietly said: 'And now before we have tea, perhaps you would like to see the apartments of the Lady in whom you take so great an interest; you are standing now in what was her dining room, and now come upstairs and I will show you her bedroom.

So this was his little surprise for us and of which he had given no hint even in his letter. Yes, he himself occupied the royal apartments of Queen Anne Boleyn, and we had our afternoon tea in her drawing-room. I may seem to be telling fairy tales and so they are, but there is this added charm about them that they are all true and did not happen long ago in days of old when knights were bold, but in our own prosaic days of railway tickets and taxi-cabs.

And so within the same year the three great castles had opened their gates and no one was more surprised than myself, for had I been told that such a thing would have happened, I certainly would not have believed it possible.

I very much wished that I knew someone who could show me where the old royal palace at Greenwich stood, and the site of the tilt yard where Sir Henry Norris and Lord Rochford had contended under the eyes of that poor May Queen who was already doomed.

It all came about quite simply. Shortly after my visit to Windsor we were asked to take in for a month or so a little girl called Audrey, as we had also a little girl, Lilian, to whom she would be a companion.

Audrey's parents might have lived anywhere else of course, but they happened to live at Greenwich, and her father happened to be an instructor in the Royal Naval College, and so they just happened to live on the site of the old Pacentia Palace, the home of the Lady Anne, and so of course her father drew me out plans of the place, showing me the position of the tilt yard, etc., and sending me a warm invitation to see it all for myself, which of course I did.

What could be more simple and natural, but I wonder mathematically what were the probabilities against it, and whether any fairy story is really more wonderful.

Here within a year all my wishes had been fulfilled, and I

had been invited by complete strangers to all the places which I had set my heart on going to and indeed to every spot in England specially connected with the Lady Anne Boleyn, except her supposed birthplace at Blickling Hall, Norfolk, which I was not so desirous to see as the old house where some say she was born does not now exist.

CHAPTER THREE

CLAIRVOYANCE

'We are compassed about with a great cloud of witnesses, hidden from us by only a thin veil, which at any moment may be rent asunder.'

BISHOP WILKINSON.

Naturally I often wondered whether all these happenings and coincidences were purely accidental or whether my prayer had indeed been granted. I could see no means by which this could ever be known on earth, when an experience came to me which was as unexpected as it was unsought. On August 19th, 1921, I got an urgent letter from my sister Mary in Bournemouth asking me to come and meet a friend who was on a short visit to Bournemouth, with whom was staying a lady who was said to have great clairvoyant powers, as possibly we might be able to throw some light on the problem, though my sister doubted this possibility as much as I did myself. However, as I wished very much to see my sister, I cycled down from Farnham through the beautiful New Forest, and the next day at 10 a.m., my sister's friend Mrs Andrews, came bringing with her the clairvoyant lady Mrs Clegg. I should say here that Mrs Clegg was not a professional clairvoyant, that she knew nothing of me or my play, and practically nothing about the Tudor period, and was about 60 years of age. I entered into conversation with Mrs Clegg in the well lighted drawing room and she told me that her mother had possessed clairvoyant powers and that though she did not make use of them publicly, her family had never known her mistaken in what she described. Then Mrs Clegg discovered, even as a child, that she too had a similar gift, but said that she had not used it either, because when she grew up and was married, she was too occupied with domestic affairs, having a

13

large family to attend to. In the middle of the war, 1914–1918 however, she had a wonderful vision. She saw our Lord standing in the shadow of a cross, with a look of great compassion upon His face, and He said to her 'My daughter, I want you now to use your great gift to comfort those who are in sorrow'. This she regarded as a sacred commission, and as her family was now grown up, she felt free to go to those who called her or who needed her. It was her joy to be of any use to bring comfort at her Lord's desire to the many in grief and suffering and often in despair through their losses in the war.

She spoke on for quite a quarter of an hour, telling of the way her husband had been won by her clairvoyancy from indifference to faith in Christ before he died, and then she quietly said, without any change in her voice or expression: 'As we have been speaking, a figure has stole in and is standing beside you. He is very tall and erect. I should say about 60 years of age. He has white hair and a broad forehead: a nose a little broad at the base, and a small beard. He has very high spiritual powers and impresses you very much in your work. Can you place him?'

I replied: 'No, I am afraid I cannot, as I don't know anyone of that appearance.' Then a sudden idea came to me and I said: 'It may be some historical person whom I have never seen. Ask him, has he a daughter?'

'He is nodding his head. Yes, he has a daughter.'

P.W.   'Can he describe his daughter?'
C.   'He may not be able to describe her. That may not be possible.'

Then after a moment's pause: 'There is a lady now standing between us; it is his daughter. She is medium height: I should say about 28 or 30. She is finding it difficult to build herself up. Is this the first time she has appeared to you?'

P.W.   'Yes.'
C.   'Well, that probably accounts for it. She has beautiful hair and an oval face; she has hazel brown eyes; she is very vivacious and quick, and I should say is very musical and poetical, she wears a necklace. She has very good teeth and a beautiful neck and figure. She has good

hands, rather plump. She is very well dressed in a quaint low dress, and is very careful about her dress and likes light colour. She is standing in a garden. Does that convey anything to you?'

It was of course a perfect description of the Lady Anne Boleyn, but though I was surprised I simply said:

'Yes, I think so; may I ask a question?'

'Yes.'

'Can she tell me of any mark on her hands by which I could recognise. her?' (A mark on her little finger.)

'I think it would be better not to make a definite suggestion like that. She might have given it if you had not asked for it. It is better to ask her for a sign and not suggest what form the sign shall take.'

'Well can she tell me her name?'

'She is laughing now. She says "A rose by any name would smell as sweet".'

I had called her in the play 'The Rose of Kent', a name peculiarly my own for her, indeed I had been thinking of calling the play 'Anne Boleyn, or the Rose of Kent', but it was not the answer I expected, nor did the appropriateness and beauty of the reply, so very characteristic of her strike me till later.

P.W. 'Can she now tell me anything about herself and who she was?'

C. 'We are moving away now from the garden. It seems like a court. Oh (with great surprise), she is a royal personage. But I feel a great emotion. Oh, there is something very sad here; she did not live long; she passed over very suddenly. Oh, but there was a tragic ending; oh, the emotion; something in the blood, was it fever? Oh no, it was something terrible; what was it? It is all blood, blood! There was a terrible tragedy. She says not to think of it now; she does not think of it; it is all past, and she wants you to know that her life now is very real and happy. She wants your hand. (Here Mrs Clegg grasped mine firmly.) She wants to impress upon you the reality of her life now and the great interest which she takes in you. She wants to impress this upon you, the reality of her present life and that there are more things in Heaven and earth than are dreamt of in your philosophy. (A pause.) Oh, there is something very strange here; she is in some way identified with you. There is some affinity of soul. She says "two in one". She is a great deal to you. She wants your hand again. She wants you to understand this, it is her special message. Does this help you?'

I did not want Mrs Clegg to know of whom she was speaking or to give her any clue, so I simply said:

P.W.   'Yes, I think so. I am doing some special work for her, does she know about it?'

C.   'Yes, she is greatly interested in it. She is very pleased with your work for her and says "successful, successful".'

P.W.   'Can she tell me what kind of work I am doing for her?'

C.   'I see groups of people moving about. Does this help you?'

P.W.   'Yes, it has to do with groups of people.'

C.   'They are all moving in and out; many groups of people.' (The play! But I did not say so.)

P.W.   'Is she quite satisfied with my work?'

C.   'Yes, she is very pleased; she says that you must be analytical in your work, but not super-analytical.

P.W.   'Can she give me any sign by which I might know her?'

C.   'She gives you as a sign, a white rose. Does that mean anything?'

P.W.   'Yes, a great deal.'

In the play I first represent her as a May Queen crowned with white roses; then the red Tudor Rose with its sorrow enters into her life, but at the end of Act II, she is seen looking into the distant future when her daughter Elizabeth is queen, and she sees herself once again crowned with the white roses only.

> The mother is forgotten in the child,
> But in the hearts of all the best of men
> Her memory lives, and in Westminster's halls
> Her statue stands, they call her Queen of May;
> And on her head they place a crown of flowers,
> Not white and red, but only white, a pure
> White crown of roses which shall never fade.
>   Act II. Scene 4.

What more suggestive and beautiful sign could have been given than a white rose, though I was expecting the mark on her finger. Quite clearly, Mrs Clegg was not just reading my mind.

C.   'Yes, white roses. She is lingering on; she seems to stay with you. She is smiling. She is not leaving you. She is very closely attached to you.'

P.W.   'Do you know the person you have been describing?'

C.   'No.'

P.W.   'Well, you have described a historical figure who lived hundreds of years ago, and you have described her to the very life. Shall I tell you who it was?'

C.   'If you like, but I know very little about history and probably should not know anything about it.'

P.W.   'Well, then, I won't tell you her name now, but you would know it if I did. Is there no name she can give me that I would know?'

C.   'She gives the name Mary. Does that mean anything?'

P.W.   'Yes, but Mary is a very common name. She had a sister called Mary. Can she tell me anything about her sister?'

C.   'She says that she was not in very close affinity with her sister on earth and she wants you to know that all that difference between them has passed away and that there is now perfect affinity between them. Does that convey anything to you?'

P.W.   'Yes, perhaps so.'

C.   'Well, she wants you to know that they are in perfect affinity now.'

This as a test of her personality was amazing, for though I said 'Yes, perhaps so', I had only the haziest remembrance of any difference between the sisters. On looking it up later, however, I found that Mary Boleyn had greatly offended her royal sister by marrying as her second husband, Sir William Stafford, a match which the King also thought beneath the dignity of the Queen's sister. It is a very minute and personal detail of the family history, and if I had read about it, I had quite forgotten it.

P.W.   'Could she tell me anything about her brother; could she give me his name?'

C.	'I catch the name William.'
P.W.	'No.'
C.	'Robert.'
P.W.	'No.'
C.	'Henry.'
P.W.	'No, I don't think so.' I thought this was just guessing. Then in a very strong voice 'George'.
P.W.	'Yes, it was George.' George was the only brother I had ever heard of. 'Can she tell me anything about her daughter?'
C.	'I get the ideas of art and literature.'
P.W.	'Yes, perhaps so, she had to do with art and literature.'
C.	'I am travelling now over the sea; there are deep jungles; dense forests and jungles; I should imagine I must be in India.'
P.W.	'No, her daughter never went over the sea, but she was connected with those who did go over the sea and went into jungles.'
C.	'Perhaps that is it. Now she is looking down from a great height on a vast expanse of water; I don't seem to catch it very well.'

This meant very little to me at the time, but when I spoke of it later to Maud, she thought that it was a capital summary of the main features of Elizabeth's reign.

1. Art and Literature.
2. Exploration and discovery.
3. Britain's control of the sea.

Mrs Clegg left after this, but said that she had a strong impression that this meeting had been pre-arranged, and that she would be led to come again in the afternoon, and I determined that if she did, I should ask for a description of the Lady's home, for my sister and I both thought that she would never be able to guess it.

Mrs Clegg came again at four o'clock and at once said, 'I feel the same vibrations as this morning. The same spirit is present, I think I can answer any question you care to ask.'

P.W.	'I went to her home lately, could she describe her home for me?'

C.   'I am being taken to a rural part of the country. There
     are a great many trees about it, and it is a very undulating
     country. I see a castle with gardens round it. It is not con-
     nected with the present time. The castle is hidden by
     trees and cannot easily be seen, but there is a spot near
     by from which all the country can be seen. The sun
     seems shining on one side and the other is dark. There
     is a shadow over the castle, something seems to over-
     shadow it. There was a great deal of pleasure and hap-
     piness connected with the life in the castle, but there
     was also a great deal of sorrow.'

P.W. 'Yes, that is her home.' Those who know the position of
     Hever Castle will realise how accurate the description is,
     though I didn't know till afterwards of the hill from which
     the commanding view was to be obtained. It was prob-
     ably a favourite walk of the Lady Anne Boleyn.

P.W. 'Could she tell me anything about her husband?'

C.   (Putting up her hands as if to ward something off.) 'She
     does not wish to think of it; it was something very sad;
     it is now a closed book and she does not wish it opened.'

P.W. 'Is she happy now?'

C.   'Yes, she says, she's quite happy and all that is past.'

P.W. 'Is she in any way connected with me in thought at the
     Holy Communion Service?'

C.   'Yes, there is a connection; you have been led to ask that
     question; has it anything to do with the last rites before
     her death?'

P.W. 'Yes, that is the answer I wanted to get.'

The Lady Anne just before her death asked to receive the
Sacrament, and with the sacred emblems in her hands, had for
the last time protested her innocence. This is brought out in
the play, and often at my Communions, the scene comes before me.

P.W. 'Is she satisfied with my work for her or would she care
     for me to visit any special place or person in connection
     with it?'

C.   'No, go on just as you are. She is working with you, and
     the work, our work she says, will be successful.'

P.W. 'Can she tell me how long it is since she began working with me?'

C. 'She says it has been for some time, but only about a year since you became conscious of it, and her influence has impressed itself more strongly in the last six months and is increasing.'

I had not then calculated the time but found afterwards that it was just about a year since I had begun the play, about which time I was almost convinced that the many happenings and coincidences were not mere accidents.

P.W. 'When this special work (the play) is over, will she leave me, or will she always stay with me?'

C. 'She says that she does not know, but that there is a great deal of work for you to do yet and latent powers to be developed. She says that you are going to influence many people, and that you must speak more from the deeper reaches of your soul.'

P.W. 'Can she not impress herself upon me without outside help, through writing by my hand or in some other way?'

C. 'No, she will impress your thoughts and she is impressing you more and more. There seems some barrier in the way of your joining with others in this and you must work alone. Is there a barrier?'

P.W. 'No, I don't know of one.'

C. 'Well, she says there is and that you must work alone.'

P.W. 'Apart from my special work for her, can she tell me anything about my own work?'

C. 'Yes, there is some difficulty in your path at present, but you must not be anxious; it will be removed and your path will open up before you. She wants your hand (and then very earnestly). You are being watched and guarded most carefully; do not be anxious, all will come out well. (A pause.) I see something all blue. She gives you a dove as an emblem. It is the emblem of peace. You will have peace in your heart and peace in your life and all will be well. The barrier will be removed, and your path will be a path of peace.'

This message was given so earnestly and was so exactly fitted to the difficult circumstances I was then in, that I remained silent and waited. In a few moments Mrs Clegg put her hands up to her neck, first at the back and then all round and said:

C.   'Oh, there's something here at my neck; something at the back, oh, something all round; oh, such emotion. Oh, something sharp and terrible. Oh, there was some terrible tragedy. She is giving me this as a sign. I asked for some physical sign in my own body. Oh, but this is terrible; some blow on her neck which sent her suddenly out of the world. Did she hurt her neck before she died?'

P.W. 'Yes, but you are tired, had you not better rest?' (for I saw that this physical sign had tired her). And now as you have told me so much about the lady I wanted to know about, shall I tell you who she is?'

C.   'Yes, I should like to know.'

P.W. 'Well, it is Queen Anne Boleyn; the second wife of Henry VIII, who was executed by him.'

C.   'Was she? Then that was the pain I felt round my neck. I do not know much about her. You see I had a large family to attend to and had no time for anything else.'

P.W. 'Yes, she had a sad story, and I have just written a play on it.'

I then produced the play and I was explaining the point about the white rose, when Mrs Clegg smiled and said: 'She is agreeing with all you are saying; she says you have quite caught her meaning. She is very pleased; she seems to be very much indeed to you.'

P.W. 'Why should she be? What is it which draws us together?'

C.   'There is some affinity of soul. Are you musical?'

P.W. 'Yes, but not more so than hundreds.'

C.   'She was also very poetical, and I should say that you were also, and you have these gifts in common. She could probably most easily reach you on the vibrations of music.'

P.W. 'Yes, perhaps so; but is it not very wonderful that someone who lived about 400 years ago, should be able to come into such close communion with anyone at the present time.

C.   'No, why should you think it wonderful? You must remember that for them time and space do not count.'

P.W.   'Now you must go, but I should like to ask her one more
question. Was the figure you first described this morning
her father?'

C.   'She wants your hand. Yes, emphatically yes; she wants
you to know it.'

This conversation had been so quiet and simple, and as natural
as a talk between two long absent friends, that I don't think I
was as astonished as I suppose I ought to have been. I had, I
think, been gradually prepared for it by the events which had
preceded it, and also I had long suspected that all these happenings and coincidences were not merely accidental. Besides I had
been taught from childhood to believe in 'the Communion of
Saints' and in the idea of guardian angels, and knew from
Church history that this communion was no mere figure of
speech. I felt quite certain also that Mrs Clegg was not simply
reading my subconscious mind, and I know now that she is far
too good and sincere a Christian woman to practice deceit.

My real surprise was not that the Lady Anne, in whom I took
so great an interest, should be near me, but that her father
should also have been present. In the play I bring out the truth
that his daughter's misfortunes were largely due to his own
ambition, and I had a poorer opinion of him than I have since
learned I was justified in entertaining. That he should be in any
way concerned with me puzzled me, and it was for this reason
I put my last question. My wonder and doubt were evidently
seen, and hence the very emphatic assertion and reply.

CHAPTER FOUR

GLORIOUS DEVON

*'The Church of God remains under fresh forms, the
one, holy, entire family in heaven and earth.'*

F. W. ROBERTSON.

About six weeks after my interview with Mrs Clegg, I had an
engagement to keep in Devonshire, and I had also a letter from
Mrs Andrews saying that Mrs Clegg was having a holiday with
her at Sidmouth, and that if I happened to be in that part of
the country, she hoped I would come in and see them. I determined to take the opportunity and also to avoid train fares by
cycling down to Devon in stages, calling in at Sidmouth on my
way. I left Bridport for Sidmouth on St Michael and All Angels'
Day, and before starting was able to attend Holy Communion
service in the parish church at 8 a.m., and then after a glorious
ride I reached Sidmouth via Seaton at about 3 o'clock. The
moment I entered the room where Mrs Andrews and Mrs Clegg
were sitting, the latter said laughing, 'You have brought your
Lady with you'. I don't think I was surprised, but Mrs Andrews
said, 'Can you see her?' 'No,' replied Mrs Clegg, 'I cannot see
her but she is here, feel my arm.' I felt Mrs Clegg's arm and it
was all vibrating. 'But how do you know it is my Lady as you call
her,' I said. 'Oh, I know her by the vibrations, they are distinct
in every case. This is your Lady, and she is impressing me very
strongly.'

'Well,' said Mrs Andrews, 'Mr Walsh has had a long tiring
ride, and I would suggest that he would probably like some warm
water to wash his hands and then some tea, and we can talk to
his Lady afterwards.'

I naturally laughed heartily at this, but I was glad that Mrs
Andrews had such a practical turn of mind, as there are few
places like Devon for a good appetite.

After tea Mrs Clegg said, 'Your Lady is here, but let us bow our heads first for a word of prayer.

'O God, for as much as without Thee we are not able to please Thee, mercifully grant that Thy Holy Spirit may in all things direct and rule our hearts. Amen.'

C.   'Now your Lady is here, and she wants to say how very grateful she is to you for all the trouble you have taken and are taking for her. You are giving her great pleasure and she wants you to know it.'

P.W.   'I am very glad; it is a pleasure to me to help her, and please thank her for the beautiful symbol she gave me of the dove as the emblem of peace; it has been a great help to me, and I want her to know I am very grateful to her.'

C.   'She says that she knows you are grateful, and she feels it before you say it. She wants your hand. She wants to impress upon you the reality of the future life and of her life, and that joy is born of sorrow; weeping may endure for a night but joy cometh in the morning.'

P.W.   'Please ask her, does the Lord Jesus know of our meeting in this way and does He quite permit it?'

C.   'Yes, she says He knows and has allowed it to be arranged for.'

P.W.   'Has she ever seen the Lord Jesus?'

C.   'She says that she is always in His Presence, it surrounds her as with a beautiful, warm, golden light.'

P.W.   'Can you see her now?'

C.   'No, not now; she is standing behind me, but I feel her presence and I see the light she is shedding over you.'

P.W.   'Why is she taking such an interest in me?'

C.   'She says it is because of soul affinity. Where there is this soul affinity there is always this drawing together.'

P.W.   'Did she take an interest in me because I first took an interest in her, or did she create the interest and make me read the passage in the book which first aroused that interest?'

C.   'She created the interest and caused you to read the extract. She was trying to influence you for a long time before that but could make no impression.'

P.W.   'This work I am doing for her is only a small thing, a matter of a few years; will she then leave me?'

C.   'She says that she will never leave you, that where there is a soul affinity, the contact can never be broken.'

P.W.   'Shall I see her when I pass on into the other life?'

C.   'Why yes, we shall never be separated again.'

P.W.   'In what way exactly is she connected with me, is it as a guide and does she know my guides?'

C.   'Yes, she says that you have many guides, but that she is not one of your guides. She is connected with you by soul affinity, not as a guide but as a guardian angel.'

P.W.   'Why is her father helping me, is it at her suggestion?'

C.   'She says, "He is helping you because you are working for me". I get the impression that he helped to bring on the marriage which led to her troubles.'

P.W.   'Yes, that is so.'

C.   'Well, that is it; he wishes to undo the harm he did and in some way make amends for it.'

P.W.   'Did she ask him to help me?'

C.   'Yes, he came at my request.'

P.W.   'Can she tell me something of her life and work all these 400 years?'

C.   'She says her work has been to help those who have been wrongly accused and condemned. Just as you are helping her, so she has been helping others.'

P.W.   'Can she tell in what sphere she is?'

C.   'She says, the sixth sphere.'

P.W.   'Please tell her that for the sake of a test I am trying to trace her brothers' names. Would she give them to me again.'

I knew that Mrs Clegg would never remember the names which she gave six weeks previously, and I also wanted them for test purposes, as given in the chapter of Tests.

C.   'George, William, Henry, Robert, Thomas.'

These names are the same with the addition of Thomas.

P.W.   'Please thank her and tell her that I have traced Thomas and Henry and probably William but I cannot find Robert.'

C.   'Had she a brother who died very young?'

P.W.   'I think she had, I think he was buried in the chancel of Hever Church just beside her father and the spot is marked by a small cross in the floor.' (This I found later and the name on it was Robert'.)

C.   'Yes she agrees, this I should say is the Robert she refers to. She also is giving you the name Elizabeth.'

P.W.   'Yes, that is of course her daughter.'

C.   'And "Mary my friend!".'

P.W.   'Yes, that is Mary Wyatt. Now can she tell me where Mary Wyatt is buried?' (I asked this as a possible test, but of course Mary Wyatt died after the Lady Anne and so in any case she would hardly know where she was buried.)

C.   'She says, "Why seek the living among the dead".'

P.W.   'I only asked it as a test. Can she give me any information unknown to me the truth of which I could verify?'

C.   'I see her now standing beside a beautiful white horse; it has velvet on the saddle; it was a favourite horse; it has a beautiful mane. There is some kind of canopy over her. It has to do with some happy time in her life. I seem to see a procession.'

P.W.   'Was it going to her coronation?'

C.   'Yes. Now I see her standing by the white horse in riding costume. She is about 24 years old I should say now. There is a white, rather ordinary looking house with three stories and beautiful avenues of trees about it.'

P.W.   'Is it Blickling Hall?'

C.   'Yes.'

I gathered that the test proposed was that she had a favourite white horse on which she used to ride at Blickling Hall and that while she was carried in her coronation procession under a canopy, this favourite horse saddled with velvet, was also led to Westminster Abbey.

P.W.   'That is very difficult. I am afraid that I could never verify it. Is there a picture of this white horse in Blickling Hall?'

C.   'There was.'

P.W.   'I am afraid it is gone now. Can she suggest anything else?'

C.   'She is placing a book on your knees. It seems bound in gold. Is it a diary?'

P.W.   'No, it is her psalter.'

C.   'Yes, she had it at the end and gave it to her friend.'

P.W.   'Yes I know. Can she tell me where that book is now?'

C.   'No, she does not seem to know. I see her now holding a small dog, a small pet dog. Had she one?'

P.W.   'I don't know. She had a large greyhound named Urian, but I never heard of a small one.'

C.   'Well, she is showing it to you.' (Found later.)

P.W.   'I am afraid I could never trace that, can she suggest something not quite so difficult?'

C.   'There is a gentleman standing beside her now; he has a plume in his hat. He was connected with her in some way. I hear the name Buckingham.'

P.W.   'I don't know. I never heard of anyone called Buckingham connected with her; I will try to look it up. Does she know anything of my own father and mother?'

C.   'No, she does not seem to know them.'

P.W.   'Does she know my little girl Helen?' (Helen died in China in 1908, aged only three months.)

C.   'Yes, she knows Helen.'

P.W.   'Is Helen a child now?'

C.   'Why no! Not a child, she is grown to girlhood; she is often with you in your home among you all.'

P.W.   'Can we ever meet without a third person?'

C.   'The difficulty of meeting is great, not with her but with you. For a long time she tried to reach you and failed and now you have the same difficulty in reaching her.'

P.W.   'Is there any use trying?'

C.   'She seems to suggest that she would succeed most probably through the vibrations of music.'

C.   'She is holding up now a ring. It has an oval stone in it, it is an amethyst.'

P.W.   'Does it exist now and does she want me to find it?'

C.   'No, it seems to have been an heirloom.'

P.W.   'I am afraid as a test it is too difficult if it no longer exists.'

C.   'Now she is again showing you the white horse. There
        was some pageant in which it took part. She was carried
        with a canopy over her and there was something special
        on her head. The horse was led in the procession with a
        velvet saddle.'

P.W.   'Yes, it is her coronation. I shall look it up.'

C.   'She gives the name Buckingham again.'

P.W.   'I don't know anything about him but I shall try to find
        the connection.'

C.   'She is giving these for a purpose.'

P.W.   'I know, she is giving them for tests, but they are
        too difficult and I am afraid that I shall never trace
        them.'

P.W.   'What did she mean by a shadow over Hever Castle; was
        it the flag?'

C.   'Yes it was the flag, but it was also the shadow of life.
        She was entering into the shadow and it fell over every-
        thing.'

P.W.   'Can she say anything about my work next year; shall I
        be moving about as I am now or shall I be settled?"

C.   'You will be settled. She shows me a garden with flowers
        and you are doing literary work in it.'

P.W.   'Can you give me another symbol like the dove, which
        has been a help to me.'

C.   'Can you see the colours?'

P.W.   'No.'

C.   'Well there is blue, and now white, and now red. They
        are the royal colours of England. And now beneath them
        is an anchor. She gives you the anchor as a symbol. You
        will be anchored and kept steadfast. Now she is placing
        a mantle over your shoulders. It is a mantle of protection.
        You will always be protected. Do not be anxious. But
        she says that the dove is her special symbol to you.' (As
        I was going the next week to Ireland, I took the mantle
        of protection to be for this visit.)

P.W.   'Well, please thank her now from me for all her
        help.'

C.   'She is smiling; she is pleased; she says she will always
        help you and that her symbol for you is the dove and that

you need have no anxiety. You will be offered a parish
with the snowdrops and you will go to it with the
daffodils.'

I can perhaps partly understand, on the principals of telepathy, how the anxiety in my mind could be felt, as my time with
the Church Missionary Society would terminate at the close of
the year and I had as yet no prospect of a parish in which I could
continue to work and attend to the education of my children,
and under the circumstances a certain amount of anxiety was
bound to reveal itself, but how the Lady Anne or anyone else
either in this world or the next, could foretell the future, seemed
to me incredible and shows how little we really know of the laws
and workings of the spirit of God, for the promise was amply
fulfilled. On Christmas Day I received the offer of the parish of
Sulgrave, a place of which I had never heard, and on going to
visit it in early January 1922 the Vicarage grounds were white
with snowdrops and when we came into residence in March the
garden was so ablaze with daffodils that the old gardener who
had been there for forty years kept on ejaculating, 'Oh, them
daffodils, them daffodils, I never seen the like', nor were the
snowdrops or the daffodils ever seen again in such pro-
fusion during my time as vicar. In that 'Snowdrop Parish' we
remained for over thirty years until I retired aged eighty-seven
in 1954.

But to return to earth and to glorious Devon, I wanted to be
alone and I went for a short walk returning just before supper
and on re-entering the room Mrs Clegg exclaimed: 'Oh, your
Lady is here again, I have never seen her so plainly. She is
radiant, oh, how radiant and happy.'

I said, 'Do describe her'.

C.   'She has a soft white dress, rather low with a necklace.
      Her hands are on her lap. She has a crown of white roses
      on her head. She is radiantly happy and says that this is
      the completion of her work.'
P.W. 'Does she mean the play?'
C.   'Yes, she says it is the completion of her work and of her
      success. She says the word "satisfied". She is very grateful
      for all kindness and sympathy shown to her on the earth

      plane. Mrs Andrews, she wishes also to thank you.' Mrs
      Andrews (who had been coming in and out during the
      conversation), 'Oh, I am only too glad to help in any
      way'.

C.   'She again repeats the word "satisfied".'

And so ended a visit to Devonshire I shall not easily forget.

CHAPTER FIVE

THE TESTS

'Prove all things, hold fast that which is good.'
ST PAUL.

Although to me the statements made by Mrs Clegg seemed very wonderful and although I believed her to be genuine, still I knew that I was very inexperienced in all such matters, and that a clever clairvoyant could have picked some of what was said out of my mind or subsconscious self, and that from an evidential point of view that part of it was valueless. For instance, the description of the Lady Anne Boleyn and of Hever Castle could have been read from my mind, but on the other hand there was a good deal said that was not in my mind at all, and a certain amount which never had been in my mind and certainly had never been in Mrs Clegg's mind. The want of sympathy between the sisters, if I ever had read of it, had completely passed from my memory; the fact that the country all about Hever can be overlooked from a hill in the neighbourhood, I did not know, but verified it by an ordnance map; the summary of the characteristics of Queen Elizabeth's reign was so original that I did not even understand it without assistance, while the allusions to the play and the rose given as a symbol of her name, and the white rose as a sign by which I should recognise the speaker, were in addition to all that, the speaker had given me for test purposes, information absolutely unknown to me and which when I received it seemed quite impossible to verify. I shall include among these tests the names of her brothers, as I thought that the Lady Anne had only one brother George, and I had never heard of any others to my knowledge.

The tests were thus five in number.

First. That her brothers' names were William, Robert, Henry, Thomas and George.

Second. That she was closely connected with a man named Buckingham.

Third. That in her coronation procession, while she was carried under a canopy with something special on her head, her favourite white horse saddled with velvet was led in the procession, and that there since had been a picture of this white horse at Blickling Hall, but which she did not know if it existed now or not.

Fourth. That she possessed as an heirloom, a ring with an oval amethyst stone.

Fifth. That she possessed a small pet dog.

I confess that the task of tracing any one of these tests seemed to me hopeless.

To begin with the brothers' names:—I thought this was pure guesswork on the part of Mrs Clegg, and it had disappointed me, but when I began to study for the test, I found to my amazement that the Lady Anne Boleyn was one of a large family, and that it was not the little family of three children which I had always thought. Then I discovered that a brother Henry was interred in the family vault of Hever Church and that another brother Thomas was buried in Penshurst Chapel about seven miles away, while George was, as I knew, buried beside his sister in St Peter ad Vincula in the Tower of London.

Later on I found the name Robert on a small stone at the foot of the tomb of Sir Thomas Boleyn in Hever Church and he had evidently died as a child. William was almost certainly her eldest brother named after his grandfather Sir William Boleyn and so, the first test was practically completely verified.

The second test yielded excellent results. I found that Edward Stafford, third Duke of Buckingham (1478-1521) was very closely connected indeed with the Lady Anne Boleyn.

(1)   He lived at Tonbridge, only about seven miles from Hever and had property also at Penshurst close by, and as he constantly resided in Kent, the two families must have been

thrown much together, tho' Buckingham was Lady Anne's senior by 23 years.

(2) He married Elinor or Alianore, who was the eldest sister of the very Lord Percy to whom the Lady Anne herself was engaged.

(3) His second daughter Elizabeth married the Lady Anne's uncle, the old Duke of Norfolk, three times her own age.

(4) He must have been with the Lady Anne at the wedding of Mary Tudor to Louis XI and they probably travelled to France together.

(5) He was also with her at the Field of the Cloth of Gold in 1521.

(6) He was executed when the Lady Anne was just twenty years of age, and the death of her old friend must have made a great impression upon her, coming just as it did when she was as it were just entering upon her life. And this impression must have been deepened when her own sad death drew near, as the two tragedies closely resembled each other, for—

(a) They were both charged with attempts to kill the King.

(b) They were both tried in the month of May.

(c) They were both tried by a carefully selected body of peers, 24 in her case, 17 in his.

(d) They were both refused the right to cross examine or see their accusers.

(e) They were both sentenced by the same judge Lord Norfolk who was closely related to them both.

(f) They both maintained that they were innocent, but submitted to the King's pleasure in almost the same words.

(7) His property at Tonbridge and Penshurst was confiscated and some of it was given to her father, which probably accounts for the fact that her brother Henry was buried in Penshurst Chapel and not in Hever Church.

Of all this I was in complete ignorance when the test was given, but it proved indeed true that she was closely connected with the man named Buckingham.

The third test was much more difficult and at one time I despaired of working it out. I found that 'her own palfry' saddled with velvet had indeed been led in the procession to Westminster, and then in an old book in the home of Sir Robert Williams, in Dorset, I found a full account of the procession. The book was in my bedroom there and was a collection of Archbishop Cranmer's letters, in one of which he thus describes the procession.

> We received the Queen apparelled, in a robe of purple velvet . . . . she sitting in her chair upon a horse litter richly apparelled and four knights of the five ports bearing a canopy over her head . . . . and on her head she had a coif with a circlet about it full of rich stones.

I found this corroborated in Stow's *Annuals* in the British Museum.

I had everything now correctly except the colour of the horse. Stow's *Annuals* gave the name of the man who led the horse (Coffin). Strickland said it was 'Her own palfry', but neither high nor low could I find out the colour. Then I suddenly came upon it.

When Sir Montague Brown so kindly asked me to Windsor Castle, I drew a bow at a venture and asked him by letter whether he had ever heard the colour of Queen Anne Boleyn's favourite horse, and he wrote back, 'I have always understood that the unhappy Lady rode a *white palfry* and in the picture of her entering Henry VIII's gateway – where His Majesty received her – which I have seen she was thus mounted'.

Thus this most difficult and complicated test proved absolutely correct in every detail, and probably the picture itself was once at Blickling as the speaker had said.

But if the white horse test was difficult, the oval amethyst ring seemed absolutely impossible. The ring, probably does not exist now, at least I don't suppose so and I could find no mention of a ring in any book, while no picture that I know of shows the Lady Anne's hands, and so I gave it up.

Then suddenly to my astonishment and delight I found it in Windsor. I was one of a large party being shown through the state apartments, when in one of the rooms I saw a picture of the Princess Elizabeth aged about 13. The picture was beyond the ropes and too far for me to see clearly, but the hands were visible, and as I had already spoken to the guide of my interest in the Tudor pictures, I now asked him would he mind going over to the picture and telling me what rings were on the fingers. He very kindly stepped over the ropes and I waited anxiously.

'There is a ring with a square green stone on the first finger.'
'Thank you, what is on the next finger?'
'A similar ring with a smaller green square stone.'
My hopes sank. 'Is there a ring on the little finger?'
'Yes, on the little finger there is a ring with an oval amethyst.'
I nearly said 'Got it', aloud.

Undoubtedly it was her mother's ring, the heirloom I had been given as a test, and I ask in this case where the subconscious self theory could possibly have come in?

In September 1923, I heard the Lady Carrick a descendant of the Boleyns was reading this MSS. and pointing to a gold ring with an oval amethyst on her finger, said that it might be the very ring, as it had been handed down for generations in the family and most probably came from the Boleyns.

The fifth test, the small pet dog defeated me altogether. Had it been the big greyhound Urian, it would have been easy enough, as this dog is mentioned in Agnes Strickland's lives of the Queens of England, but then it would have been no real test as it was already in my mind. I had never heard that the Lady Anne was fond of or possessed small dogs and I could find nothing to help me either in book or picture.

About seven years later, when I had given up all hope of finding the small pet dog the fifth test, I came across an article by Miss Olga Linds in the *Tail Waggler* of April 1930, in which she said that the Lady Anne possessed a small dog called Pompadour, or Pompey as a pet name. The article went on to say that the Queen took this pet dog with her to the Tower, where it sickened and died on the eve of the execution of its mistress, and that she was so concerned about her pet that it must have helped her to forget her own sorrow.

Almost immediately after reading the article I had the story confirmed by the Vicar of Altborough, Nuneaton (Mr Rogers) with whom I was staying, he told me that this was one of the best known stories of the Tower and had been told to him forty years ago by an uncle of his who had been the Governor.

There may be some other explanation as to how these five difficult tests were given and proved to be historically verified, but to most students the simplest explanation will probably prove to be the most reasonable.

CHAPTER SIX

LONDON TOWN

'The eye of faith that waxes bright
Each moment by thine altar's light,
Sees them e'en now; they still abide,
In mystery kneeling at our side.'
       KEEBLE *(The Christian Year).*

It took me a considerable time to work out these tests, and just as I had completed them, I had an invitation from Mrs Andrews to tea with her in London, as both she and Mrs Clegg were anxious to hear how I was progressing with them.

It was on November 15th, 1921, that I was invited, and after tea at 4 o'clock as we three were sitting round the fire, Mrs Clegg said:—

'Now your Lady is here. She is very bright; she is not in the same dress as before. She seems to be in her ethereal or spiritual state. I seem to see through her as it were. She has the same oval face and brown eyes and beautiful figure, and her hands are folded as if in the attitude of prayer. Now you may ask me anything you like?'

I might say here that I think Mrs Clegg would have spoken in the same way no matter how many were present, I think she would speak in the same way if we met in the street.

P.W.   'I should like to ask her about the tests she gave me. I am finding them out. Does she know that I went last week to Windsor and was in her old rooms?'

C.   'Yes, she says she arranged for you to go.'

P.W.   'Well ask her was the ring on the Princess Elizabeth's finger in the picture in the state rooms, the ring she gave me as a test?'

37

C.	'Yes, she says it was the ring she meant.'
P.W.	'Well, tell her that I never thought I could find it.'
C.	'She says she gave it as a test, because she knew you could find it.'
P.W.	'Tell her that I have found them all out now except the little pet dog and I am afraid that I can never find that.'
C.	'She says that you will find it.'
P.W.	'I have found out a great deal about Buckingham. Would she care to tell me anything more about him to make the test complete? I don't want to trouble her if she would rather not.'
C.	'No, you have enough about him for a test.'
P.W.	'Does she know that I have found out about the white horse?'
C.	'She knows it.'
P.W.	'Isn't she pleased?'
C.	'She is smiling. She says you have done very well. She is holding up a little miniature; it is a small picture of herself; it is painted; I catch the name "Percy".'
P.W.	'Did she give it to Percy?'
C.	'Yes.'
P.W.	'Is it in existence now?'
C.	'She does not know.'
P.W.	'Does she give it as a test?'
C.	'No.'

Ten days later I was in a clergyman's house in Sheffield for tea, when behind my seat I noticed a book called *Henry VIII* by Pollard. I asked, might I look at it and there I came upon a miniature of the Lady Anne Boleyn, probably this very one referred to. I came across an enlarged copy of this miniature in Bournemouth a few months after and on my birthday in 1922, I received a beautifully enlarged copy of it from my sister.

C.	'Now she is holding up a small handkerchief; it is embroidered at one corner; it seems to be connected with something very sad, some sorrow in her life. She is holding it in her fingers and she drops it. She says it was unintentionally that she dropped it.'

P.W. 'Is it the handkerchief she dropped at the Greenwich Jousts?'

C. 'Yes, she says it was unintentionally dropped, but it brought her great sorrow.'

P.W. 'Yes, I know it did. Now if she does not mind talking about the sadder parts of her life, will she tell me if she remembers Lady Kingston? I do not want to ask her to speak of it if it in any way pains her.'

C. 'Yes, she remembers her.'

P.W. 'Can she tell me anything about her?'

C. 'She is kneeling now and putting her head on my knees.'

P.W. 'Yes, now can she say why she is doing so?'

C. 'I catch the word "sorroe" . . . . "sorry". It was about someone else, about some child.'

P.W. 'Yes, it was about a child.' (Here Mrs Andrews who had gone out came in again and hearing the mention of a child said, 'I suppose she is speaking of her child, Elizabeth'.)

P.W. 'No, it is not Elizabeth, she is speaking about the Princess Mary.'

C. 'She says, "Sorry, Sorry", and I get the idea of some commission connected with it.'

P.W. 'Yes, she asked Lady Kingston to go to the Princess Mary and tell her she was sorry for not treating her more kindly.'

C. 'Yes, and she says Lady Kingston did it, she did it.'

P.W. 'I know she did.'

C. 'She says that after passing over, she had to go through a period of sorrow and remorse and then she came through it all into her present joy.'

P.W. 'Is she perfectly happy now?'

C. 'Yes, perfectly happy.'

P.W. 'Does it trouble her to speak of her life on earth?'

C. 'No, that is all passed, she can think of it now without pain.'

P.W. "Now I want to ask about my work. I have finished the play and what is the next work I am to do?'

C. 'You will be guided as to the next work.'

P.W. 'But am I to tell my experiences in connection with the play?'

C. 'You are to make known the deeper truths which you have been taught. I seem to see a great deal of writing; there is evidently a great deal for you to do.'

P.W. 'Am I to do it at once?'

C. 'You will be guided as to when to do it.'

P.W. 'Now will you tell her that I have been trying to do what she said and to speak from the deeper reaches of my soul.'

C. 'She says she knows you have and that you are being greatly used and will be used to help others still more. She says you are developing rapidly; the coarser vibrations are becoming finer and love is ruling your heart.'

P.W. 'May I ask again about this affinity of soul she spoke of. I don't quite understand. How can someone who lived 400 years ago have this affinity with someone living on earth now?'

C. 'She says, "Time is nothing and space is nothing". Soul affinity is independent of them.'

P.W. 'Still, one would have thought that soul affinities would have been born in the same era on earth.'

C. 'Not necessarily, in many cases soul affinities never meet on the physical plane. She is showing me links of gold. She says that you are bound together with links of golden love. Love is the great uniter and it is love that underlies soul affinity.

> Love is kind and suffers long,
> Love is meek and thinks no wrong,
> Love than death itself more strong,
> Therefore bound by Love.'

P.W. 'Can she tell me something about her life and her work now, I mean apart from the play, her own special work?'

C. 'She says that she cares for not-wanted children and Magdalens . . . . Magdalens. She goes down to their dark regions to help these poor Magdalens.'

P.W. 'Does she mean on the earth?'

C. 'Not on earth; on this side.'

P.W. 'Does she go alone?'

C.   'Not alone, others go with her.'

P.W.   'Well, if I am in affinity with her shall this be my work too?'

C.   'She says, you will co-operate with her.'

P.W.   'But I don't see how that is possible. She is in the sixth sphere she says, and when I cross over I shall be in a very humble sphere. How can I possibly co-operate with her?'

C.   'She says, when you leave the physical body, you will progress very rapidly and you will soon reach her sphere.'

P.W.   'But then I am afraid that I shall be keeping her back.'

C.   'That is impossible; that will not keep the soul back.'

P.W.   'Can you see her still?'

C.   'Yes, quite plainly: she is very bright and in her spiritual robes.'

P.W.   'If she is so close to me, can she not touch me or in some way make me feel her presence?'

C.   'She can only touch you through your mind.'

P.W.   'Can she never appear to me until I see her beyond the veil?'

C.   'She says that she will ask for this concession that you may be able to see her before you leave the physical plane.'

P.W.   'Does she know if I shall leave the physical plane soon?'

C.   'She says you have a great deal of work to do on earth yet and many latent powers to be developed.'

P.W.   'Can I help her in any way to appear to me?'

C.   'Yes, by prayer.'

P.W.   'She said before that the vibrations of music would help her.'

C.   'Yes, music and poetry.'

P.W.   'Now I must soon be going and I have asked about all the questions I wanted to, but before I go is there anything special she wants to say to me?'

C.   'She wants your hand. She says that you are to remember that joy is born of sorrow and that out of trouble springs happiness. She is showing me a star, it is wonderfully bright and scintillating at all the points, very brilliantly.

She says "The Star of the East". The darkness is passing
from the earth and the dawn appeareth.

> O'er the earth the morn is breaking,
>   Dawn is chasing back the gloom,
> And the sons of men are waking,
>   from the shadows of the tomb.'

P.W.   'But some say that this is not so and that the earth is
growing worse and going to destruction.'

C.   'No, no, it is not so. The light is shining over the earth
for the coming of the Christ.'

P.W.   'Do you mean that He is coming again in person?'

C.   'He is coming into the hearts of men and bringing into
their lives, love and peace and unity.'

P.W.   'But when our Lord ascended, the angels said He would
so come in like manner.'

C.   'He comes in person into the hearts of men. It is to be
taken in its deeper sense. It is the deeper truth which
underlies the words which you must seek for.

> God's in His Heaven,
>   All's right with the world.'

P.W.   'Who is your greatest friend in Heaven?' I fully expected the reply Mary Wyatt and had Mrs Clegg been
reading my mind she would have said so, but the answer
was:—

C.   'Christ is the greatest Friend. He is the great eternal
Friend of all here.'

P.W.   'Yes, of course. How beautiful! Do you sometimes see the
Lord Jesus?'

C.   'Yes, sometimes, but not at all times.'

P.W.   'Now I must go, but when we separate are you always still
with me and do you see me all the time?'

C.   'No, not always with you.'

P.W.   'But always when I need you?'

C.   'Yes, always when I am needed.'

P.W.   'Shall I meet you again?'

C.   'Yes, if necessity arises.'

P.W.   'How can you work with me here and still carry on your
work in Heaven. Do you leave it to come to me?'

C.	'No; thought is quicker than the bird's wing. The two things are quite possible; you will understand when you come here.'
C.	'Now she is taking her robe and with the hem is covering us both; it is for protection. Do you feel my arm vibrating all over?'
P.W.	'Yes.'
C.	'She is impressing me very powerfully; I seem as it were lifted up to her plane.'
P.W.	'Can she appear in any dress she wishes?'
C.	'Yes.'
P.W.	'Has she a crown of roses on her head?'
C.	'No, she is not in her earth garb. She is in her spirit robes, very bright and beautiful.'
P.W.	'Will she crown herself now with a wreath of white roses?'
C.	'She has done so. She is bowing very graciously. She has gone.'

CHAPTER SEVEN

THE STILL SMALL VOICE

Time passed on and I had been over a year in the Snowdrop Parish and, indeed, had practically concluded that my experiences had been just given me in God's great mercy to help me in a very special crisis of my life, and had now come to a close, when on the 1st day of December, 1922, I received the following letter from Miss Eleanor Kelly. I had met her once or twice and I knew that she had psychic gifts and was a very devout Christian woman, a member of the Church of England, and interested in my story. The letter ran as follows:

Dear Mr Pakenham-Walsh,

On the 12th of this month I was sitting as I usually do for a quiet hour in the early morning and received a message in which you and Mr Bligh Bond are both mentioned. I sent it to Mr Bligh Bond and he very kindly put it in type for me when he sent it back, so I enclose the script typed for you to read. Will you kindly send it me back. I have had some communication now and again with souls who died in the same period as Henry VIII, and I am very much interested in the reference to him and the Lady Anne and the need still for forgiveness on her part and reparation on his. It seems long, but the *time* does not appear to have anything to do with soul growth, does it? Do tell me if you are ever able to speak to the Lady Anne about this.

Yours sincerely,
Eleanor B. Kelly.

Script received by E.K. Nov. 12th, 1922.

THE SCRIPT

'As one (who) waking late from the heavy sleep of slothful self-indulgence, there stands beside thee, sister, a soul but slowly stretching itself after long and heavy slumber. Speak to him.'

E.K. 'Friend, who are you? Can I help you?'

'He answers not. Yet speak again. Thy voice echoes faintly in the locked chamber of his soul. Speak once more.'

E.K. 'Friend, I want you to tell me who you are and why have you come to speak to me.'

'He looms out of the past, a shadowy figure and a sad hearted one. Tell the Brother of Glaston that here is one who waits to unburden a sore heart; one who on earth oppressed his fellows and made havoc of the lives associated with his own. Now, at long last, the spark of Love Divine glows dimly in the ashes of his soul. Fan it into flame, that the refuse of the wicked and wasted life may be eaten by its heat, burnt up and transformed. There is reparation to be made, ere ever the soul can rise. Help thou to provide opportunity to bring about repentance and forgiveness.

Not without reason are the men and women who lived and sinned and suffered in the past brought into living communion with other souls in the present. All life is one. All history the same scroll unrolling down the ages. Yes, sister and friend, thou dost surmise aright. He whom we would bring to repentance is the evil doer of the time of another of whom thou knowest.

Beg of her sweet charity, pure forgiveness, compassionate love; Anne and Henry and yet another sinister figure of those dark days – the priest, the cardinal, he – Wolsey as men name him.

Thou art less clear than I would wish; but write to the Glaston Brother and to him to whom the woman's soul has turned for help to clear her name.

Peace and the blessing of the Sabbath Day rest on this tiny village.'

'One of the Band.'

Not thinking that such a request would lead to anything, I did not keep a copy of my reply, but fortunately Miss Kelly kept my

letter, and I am now able to produce it as it shows how dubious
and sceptical I was about the whole proposition and from the
psychic point of view is important as showing that the idea did
not originate in any way with me or because of my interest in
the Tudor people.

Thorpe Mandeville Rectory,
Banbury.

Dec. 4th, 1922 A.D.

Dear Miss Kelly,

The Script, which I return with many thanks, raises such
great trains of thought that I shall find it difficult to express
them fully in a letter, and where shall I begin?

It seems such a solemn thing to know so much and to be
even a possible agent in such a wonderful and mysterious subject. I have not even allowed Henry a place in my Tudor corner. The Lady Anne is in the centre, and all the great Tudor
people round her, but I could not put up in that corner the
face of the man who murdered her.

I only once referred to him to her, at my very first meeting,
when I was trying to establish her identity, and she put up her
hands and said she did not wish the subject referred to as she
wished it to be 'a closed book'. So I never alluded to it again.

But sometimes I cannot help thinking of him and now comes
this message about them both. It seems so strange and wonderful and I want to know why the message is sent to me, and who
sent it. It opens up such problems. The Lady Anne does not
wish to speak of him, at least she did not on the only occasion
I did so, and anyway why does not, or cannot, this messenger
approach her himself about it.

It seems so odd to appeal to her through someone else on
earth, when it would seem to me far simpler to make the appeal
direct.

Of course I should speak to her about it if I was sure that
God wished me to do so and that it was the ordained way, but
it seems to me such a strange method to go round by earth to
reach him and I wish your messenger would explain this problem and procedure and tell me who has commissioned him to
ask such a wonderful and solemn duty of me.

That is one great problem which presents itself.

And there is another. The Lady Anne says she is perfectly
happy and is in the sixth sphere. Surely no one can be perfectly
happy and so far advanced unless they already have the forgiving spirit. Of course forgiveness cannot be expressed until
repentence is expressed, but the Lady Anne, by the very fact

of her position in Heaven, must have a heart ready to forgive him or anyone else, and there can be no need to ask her to forgive or for her 'pure forgiveness'.

What must be wanted is for Henry to express his sorrow and repentance to her or so that it may reach her, and then I take it she will be ready at once to help him in any way she can.

Once when with Mrs Clegg Cardinal Wolsey came and the Lady Anne met him, he was very miserable and dejected and then I asked the Lady Anne later on if she had seen him, and she said, 'I brought him'. Then I asked if the meeting with her had helped him and she said 'Immensely'. But can they not meet except on the earth plane through a human medium? If Henry wants to express his sorrow to the Lady Anne can he not do so, without a similar meeting place on the earth plane. You see what very big questions arise and I should indeed like to know more and why this message was sent to me. Is it possible that I am to be the one to reconcile them? It seems too mysterious and wonderful even to suggest.

I very seldom now have an opportunity of meeting the Lady Anne, not being psychic myself, but two weeks ago I had to go to town and met Mrs Clegg at tea, and the Lady Anne came and brought with her my little daughter Helen who died in 1908 when she was only three months old. It was very beautiful – a number of children came singing with the Lady Anne decked with garlands of flowers, and then she led Helen to me . . . , but , , , , but I am very seldom in town and am very busy.

It was very kind of you to write and I thank you very much. The Lady Anne has told me that she does rescue work sometimes, so I suppose it would be possible for her to seek Henry.

Oddly enough on the Sunday before your letter came, as I was saying the words 'He pardoneth and absolveth all those that truly repent', etc., my thoughts seemed to go right beyond the little church and I said them louder so that if any were listening unseen they might hear, so as to possibly help unseen souls in trouble, an odd thing for an Evangelical like me to do.

What a wonderful gift you have. I should so much like to hear again from you should this messenger see the problems which his message to me has raised, and wishes to say more to me.

I am willing to speak to the Lady Anne if it is God's will and then if it is she will be prepared also and so I shall not displease her or do harm; but in such things one needs very clear guidance.

What a mysterious life we live in and how sacred it makes even one's thoughts.

We like our work here immensely, of course no one here knows of my interest in this whole subject; it would not be understood and there is no need for it. The congregations are increasing and we shall value your thought and prayer.

> With kind regards,
> Yours sincerely,
> W. S. Pakenham-Walsh.

The reply to my letter.

December 10th, 1922.

In answer to the earnest questioning of the man in Holy Orders to whom thou hast delivered our message in respect to the dark soul of the wrongful husband of the woman for whom he feels so great and true a sympathy, tell him . . . . (I failed to catch the name, it was like Alfred) . . . . is but one of a company of spirit messengers whose task, a heavy one, is to open lanes in the locked ice of the minds and souls of men.

We would indeed that all should find that pole of their being which is ever in magnetic contact with the source of all life. The planet Earth is not in perfect poise, not answering with unerring constancy to the force which keeps her in her orbit, but as she is drawn unconsciously and inevitably nearer the true relation to the sun of this system, even so is it with the race upon her bosom; the great currents play ever around all souls, according to Law, and when the indwelling spirit is released sufficiently from the covering matter which enshrouds it in its passage, the at-onement is instantaneous. Even as a drop of mercury broken into a thousand fragmentary globules will instantly coalesce again when the fragments draw near enough to feel the magnetic influence which draws them together as a whole, so is it with the myriads souls of men, one in many fragments. As all who touch the lives of others intimately must at least remove *all* that obstructs their unity, so must these two souls be cleared each alone, and each in unison, before they too take their places in the great structure of the Body of Christ.

Anne has even still some shadows to let fall before her vision is clear; he, Henry, is but now beginning to be vaguely conscious of his need of cleansing.

We would explain to the man of earth this matter of the rescue of such degraded ones. Did we, as he suggests, bring before Henry in spirit as he now is, the bright form of the woman, deeply wronged, one only among many as deeply wronged as she, her presence would be unfelt by him and her forgiveness he could not receive. To him she would still be but a ghost, one of the forms of intangible and haunting of the nightmare shadows which surround him. It is of the mercy of the loving kindness of the Father that we and you on earth can minister to such together.

I will endeavour to make this clearer in another writing, thou hadst best cease for this day. I bless and pray with and for thee sister, that thou fail not in thy part and sign my name . . . .

(Again I failed to get it clearly, E.K.)

The following night, December 11th, I (E.K.) heard the name 'Alwyn' several times repeated, and I saw a high rocky cliff (a coast cliff because I saw the sea through a chasm) with a very steep path winding up to an entrance of some kind, the hill was so steep that in parts steps were cut on the path, and I wondered if it led to a monastery, but then I saw a woman looking up the path before climbing it. After that I saw the inside of a castle and a long table with both men and women sitting at it, in old Saxon dress like pictures out of Ivanhoe. I felt pretty sure the name was the one I had failed to catch the day before and in the morning of the 12th the same spirit took up the writing at once :

'Thou hast heard and seen aright sister, my name is Saxon Alwyn, and I lived on earth long prior to the man whose soul we seek to rescue even now, long after he too has left the plane of earth.

The mysteries of time, as thou callest it, and of growth, and the awakening which ever precedes growth in spiritual knowledge, are hidden by ignorance and prejudice and creeds of man's devising. Bid the priest of whom we ask a service ever strive to keep clear in the crystal chamber of the soul the mirror of reception, that no cloud or shadow of man's own reason or belief dim the vision which shall reveal Truth to such as seek it with prayer and constancy.

More will aid him than he will wot of, in the temple of faith which holds him now. Light and understanding will inspire his teaching when he unites with souls released and enlightened for the same service of the same Lord God, the Supreme.

Those who stand apart, set to be channels of teaching, have indeed and indeed great need of humility, of brotherly love, of that wide all-embracing sympathy, which sees in the sins and sorrows and repentances of other and weaker brethren but the broken pieces of the mirror of the soul, distorting all reflections caught upon fragments too shattered and stained of the dust wherein they lie, to give any guidance. It is even in the picking up and piecing together of these broken mirrors that we seek the aid of still embodied man.

Earth's thoughts and ways are all the soul yet realises and thus it often is that we fail to make appeal to the one in need of our aid, for lack of any response; such hear us not and see us not, and we must wait, but in our waiting to answer the first faint call for help we can seek means to bring the spirit where some javelin of sight or sound may stir a memory or start a questioning train of thought, as it has been with this Henry.

We have carried his sodden soul to centres where some voice may penetrate or some sight startle him awake.

The germ of parental Love is very faintly aglow in his heart, and it is even through the child born of their union on earth that we hope to reach him. The unborn child also radiant and unstained as is the other by earth's faults, keeps watch beside his mother (i.e. the Lady Anne) to stir the compassion for his father in her heart.

She is a sweet woman and happy and she serves many, but the pages of the past must be turned. Alas, no one may *close* the book of life; some may turn aside when another with whom the page was written calls for help to wash away its stains with tears of bitter penitence. Pray for means to be found to bring this sorry spirit into peace.

Cease and I thank thee. God bless all and unite all in His service of Love.

Alwyn, once a Thane of Sussex.

CHAPTER EIGHT

THE SECOND MESSENGER – LOIS

I heard nothing more for some six months. I just kept the matter in my mind, but there was evidently nothing which could be done, and I was quite determined to take no step without some fairly clear guidance.

But on July 2nd I received the following letter from Miss Kelly, which made the work required of us a little more definite.

July 1st, 1923.

Dear Mr Pakenham-Walsh,

I am sending a message I received yesterday to Mr Bligh Bond to read and send on to you, as I have mislaid your address. I am writing from Bath but shall be in London about July 15th for a night or two. But we are not likely to be all three in town and free and with time to arrange a meeting at present I am afraid.

I am quite willing if and when you two are. Alwyn has twice tried to speak to me but I have failed to catch his words and then Lois was sent to give his message I think. I am so constantly in fresh places and disturbed and I know I often fail in my part because of the difficulty of keeping a quiet hour every day.

With kind regards and hoping all is well with you and your family and Parish.

Sincerely yours,
Eleanor Kelly.

The following is the message, preceded, as is often the case with Miss Kelly, by a vision.

June 30th, 1923. 5.30 a.m.

THE VISION

I was aware of a lot of lilies of the valley growing and of white heather, quantities of it, and there were little crowns of wreaths of the heather lying on its branches. I asked who was showing me the lillies and then this message was written.

THE MESSAGE

'It is I, Lois, I sister, that was once that butterfly soul, the vain child of a vain age, but who awoke long since in these realms of glorious life to a better understanding and a wider sympathy. Wilt listen while I speak?'

E.K. 'Yes.'

Lois. 'Then, sister, listen to the request of one whose little humble messenger I am, that one so grand and fair and clear a spirit, who descends to where I dwell that his help may be given forth for the blinded soul of the King, poor puppet, of my days on earth.

'Little of Kingly quality was there in his tarnished and tawdry mind, much alas of evil and self-will and cruelty and pride, much of vice and wickedness. But now after so long sloth is the spark beginning to glow in his heart and Alwyn, beautiful and good, has taken charge of this soul to lead him step by step upon the path of repentance and reparation.

'It is desired that thou and the Brother of Glaston and the Irish Priest, so kind and helpful to Anne, shall meet and talk of these realms together, if haply Anne and Henry may be brought within reach and recognition of each other, and Elizabeth the Virgin Queen, their daughter of the flesh, be brought also.

'The brother beloved of Anne (i.e. George, Lord Rochford) and the son so desired of her, are together weaving a shelter wherein these souls may meet.

'Part of the structure only earth can build. Wilt help? Thou and these brothers, and perchance that other who was present where I came before the first time or it might be another like to her in trance mediumship, one knowing not the reason for the aid required.

'Wilt do thy part sister? Wilt ask these brothers to bear in mind the request and seek to meet as we ask?'

E.K. 'I will do all I can, Lois.'

Lois. 'Then my errand is accomplished and back I go to tell those who sent me. Bless me sister as I do bless thee, I leave my lilies at thy feet.' Lois.

With this message from Lois came the following letter from Mr Bligh Bond.

> Glastonbury,
> Somersetshire.
> July 7th, 1923.

Dear Mr Pakenham-Walsh,

At Miss Kelly's request I am forwarding the enclosed. If it were possible I should be most willing to meet and try to see what might be achieved for the good of these souls.

How are you getting on with the Anne Boleyn quest?

Kind regards and all good wishes.

> Yours sincerely,
> Frederick Bligh Bond.

(Mr Bligh Bond was the Wells Diocesan architect and so the Abbey of Glastonbury came under his care. His book, *The Gate of Remembrance* is well known, which led to the discovery and excavation of St Edmund's Chapel behind the high altar in Glastonbury Abbey.)

The desire evidently was that we three should meet with some person with psychic gifts and that such a meeting was for some reason necessary if the band of unseen workers were to achieve their purpose.

I wrote back to Miss Kelly and also to Mr Bligh Bond to say that I was quite willing to meet with them but that I did not see how it could be arranged.

We were in different parts of England and we were all busy and could not specially give up our work for such a meeting and there was the expense to be considered.

It seemed to me reasonable to suppose that if we were really needed, Alwyn and his fellow workers could arrange both the time and place for us and that the one thing needed at present on our part was a willingness to co-operate and to have the right attitude of spirit.

I went on quietly with my work but no call came, and as month after month again passed by I began to think that the whole enterprise had failed or been given up.

But whether it was a pure coincidence, as some will say, or whether it was a part of a well-ordered and carefully prepared plan, as others will consider it, the call at last did come, not with an uncertain sound, but clear and impelling, and that through the lips of one who had already been elected to be my future bishop.

CHAPTER NINE

THE CALL

National Assembly of the Church of England.
Missionary Council,
Church House,
Westminster, S.W.1.
17th Oct., 1923.

My Dear Pakenham-Walsh,

The Missionary Council is impressed with the importance of regarding the missionary education of the Home Church as one of its primary aims. The position abroad is one of abounding hope . . . . but there are still very many who have no knowledge of missionary work.

The first step which the Council is taking is to arrange for a 'school' and conference at High Leigh, Hoddesdon, Jan. 14–18.

The school will be under the chairmanship of the Bishop of Salisbury and amongst those who have promised to take part in it are Canon Storr, Mr J. H. Oldham, the Bishops of St Albans, Lichfield, St David's, Kingston and Coventry, and other leaders in the Church.

This letter is one of invitation to yourself to be with us at High Leigh, Jan. 14–18 . . . . and we are hopeful that you will see the importance of the gathering and its objective, and if you are led to arrange to be with us we shall be most thankful.

Yours very sincerely,
Cyril C. B. Bardsley.

Such an invitation I felt in any case I should not refuse, and I felt also that it might be the call for which I had been so long prepared, and looking back upon it now I am more than ever persuaded that it was, for it led to four days of earnest spiritual preparation which was probably seen to be necessary before the intensely difficult and solemn work awaiting us: but it was not until I reached High Leigh in January that I realized what a great privilege had been given to me in being among the one-hundred-and-seventeen chosen from all the dioceses in England to be at the Conference.

I spoke to my rural Dean first about it and he strongly urged me to go and then I wrote to my future bishop accepting, and also to Miss Kelly telling her that I would be in London on January 18th and would keep that day free if she and Mr Bligh Bond could meet with me.

As the meeting seemed now to be really coming out of the clouds and was probably to be a reality, I began to take the whole matter more seriously, and at each Holy Communion service during the three intervening months I remembered it in prayer.

My chief difficulty with regard to prayer for those whom we call dead is that we know so little, if anything, of their need and condition, that it is very hard to pray intelligently for them. Here, however, if the message was true, was a soul really needing assistance and to be awakened to the reality of his own need, so that one had something definite at least to go on.

The time soon passed by and meanwhile Mr Bligh Bond had made arrangements for us to meet at the house of a lady called Mrs Hester Dowden.

I was a little anxious about the arrangement as I knew nothing about Mrs Hester Dowden and had a dread of being brought into some kind of seance with a dark room, etc.

I wrote to Miss Kelly about it and told her that I would object to any such arrangement, as I had never been to such a thing and that the only psychic person I had met was Mrs Clegg who simply sat by the fire or at tea and told one what she saw and heard.

Miss Kelly said she sympathised very fully with my feelings, and that I need have no anxiety on this score, and though she herself might have chosen another sensitive, she was satisfied that Alwyn and his band would see to it that we were led aright and that no doubt Mr Bligh Bond had, unknown to himself, chosen the right person.

On January 14th I went up to London. In another hour or less I was at Broxbourne Station, and a two mile taxi drive brought me to High Leigh.

We sat down to supper at 8 o'clock, about one-hundred-and-twenty of us; Bishops, Archdeacons and Canons galore, but all men meeting with one great aim, how best to arouse more interest in the extension of the Kingdom of Jesus Christ, and how to educate the Church to her duty and responsibility.

I dwell on all this because had I chosen my own time and arranged the meeting I should naturally have gone direct from my parish to it, but as things were arranged for me, I was, as it were, taken aside for three days into a devotional and spiritual atmosphere and came to the conflict down from the mount.

*   *   *

At last the 'School' was over and the morning of January 18th, 1924, dawned. I travelled up to Liverpool Street with Bishop Price and made my way to Westminster Abbey where I was to meet Miss Kelly at 11.30. She was waiting for me and we sat down in a quiet spot to talk. She wanted specially to tell me that she had been told that if I met Mrs Clegg in the afternoon as I was planning to do, she must not be told anything about the evening meeting nor must the Lady Anne be told, nor her assistance asked. I promised that I would not do so and then arranged that Miss Kelly should meet me at Mrs Andrews' house in Kensington at 5.30, where I was going to have tea with Mrs Clegg.

Mrs Clegg, turning to me said, 'I get the impression from you today that you are in some perplexity, there is something in your mind that you are not quite sure about, some rather mysterious and perhaps difficult problems before you. Is this so?'

'Yes,' I said. 'It is so, but I am afraid I cannot tell you what it is, I have been specially told not to do so.'

'Well, the Lady Anne is here now; she is brighter than before, she seems to have evolved spiritually and to be in a higher sphere.'

P.W.   'Then she must be in the 7th sphere.'

C.   'She does not say.'

P.W.   'A book of her life has just been published by Mr Philip Sergeant and it raises some rather interesting questions. Can she remember how old she was at her death?'

C.   'She does not reply.'

P.W.   'I ask it because there is a dispute about it and I want to get it correctly.'

C. 'She does not seem to remember. Time measurements and
dates seem to count for so little in the spirit world and
she evidently cannot recall it. She says that she is with
those whom she loved best on earth and with the friend
who was faithful to her to the last . . . . Mary Wyatt.'

P.W. 'Then it was Mary Wyatt who was with her at the end.'

C. 'Yes, my friend Mary Wyatt.'

(This is very striking. Sergeant in his big new life just published
at 18/- questions this and I had meant to ask it and then forgot
it. The lady Anne, though unable to give her age, evidently saw
this other question had been in my mind and forgotten and so
answered it with out my asking it.)

P.W. 'If she has evolved spiritually and is in a higher sphere
does that mean that she is further removed from me.'

C. ' "No," she says, "the union once established will never
be broken until you meet in the spiritual life." Why does
she show me these seals?'

P.W. 'I know the reason.'

C. 'Now I see a book sealed, what does it mean? It is a
symbol.'

P.W. 'Yes, it is a symbol, and I understand it and I shall not
speak on the subject unless she wishes it, but please ask
her if she knows about the meeting tonight and whom I
am to meet with.'

C. 'Yes, she knows. I hear the name Glastonbury, now I see
monks walking about and now there is someone ex-
cavating.'

(This, of course, was Mr Bligh Bond.)

P.W. 'Tell her I have promised not to tell her about my work
tonight, but I have been called to undertake it in a very
wonderful way and as she already knew about it, will she
tell me if I am doing what is right?'

C. 'She says you are doing what is right and what has been
arranged.'

P.W. 'Will she help me tonight?'

C. 'She will be there and help if she can. She is now placing
a roll of paper on your knees and I see you writing a
great deal.'

P.W. 'Does she mean that I am to add an account of this work on to my story?'

C. 'Yes, you have understood her meaning.'

P.W. 'Is it to be published?'

C. 'No, not at present. She is very radiant and has a circlet of white roses on her head, and she is giving you as a symbol a dove sitting on a silver circle (*i.e.* perpetual peace) and she is also showing you a gold scintillating cross. Now she is showing you an anchor and she says that you have developed spiritually and are being more and more firmly anchored in the truth.'

P.W. 'Is she still my guardian angel, now that she has ascended into a higher sphere?'

C. 'She says the union which has been formed will never be broken. I see now above her head four large letters L.O.V.E. She says that Love is the greatest power in life and controls all the spheres.'

'Now your little daughter has come and she says that she is often helping her mother and wishes to send her her love. She is very vivacious and bright eyed, I should say about fourteen or fifteen.' (Correct, died 1908.)

P.W. 'Can she give me the names of her brothers?'

C. 'I get the name Willy (her eldest brother and the only one who remembers her). Now I get the name Lois, Lois she says, she has come with Helen and is going to help you tonight.'

(This was perfectly amazing. The name Lois only comes into this story as a messenger sent by Alwyn. Of course Mrs Clegg had never heard of her and it never occurred to me that she was going to help, in fact I had never thought of her again.)

C. 'Lois says that all is ready and that all you are doing is right and you must have no fear: she says, "Fear not".'

After this Mr Thomson left, and at 6.30 Miss Kelly came to call for me, and at 7 o'clock we bade Mrs Andrews and Mrs Clegg good night and good-bye, assured of their prayers and sympathy as we fared forth to we hardly knew what.

CHAPTER TEN

CHELSEA

As WE left the bus at Chelsea Town Hall, Miss Kelly said to me, 'I was told this afternoon that we were to pray together before the meeting, and if possible in a Church'; so after locating the house where we were to meet we went to look for the old church of Chelsea which I had once before visited.

'I am afraid it will be closed at this late hour,' said Miss Kelly, 'but there is no harm trying.'

To our astonishment and joy the Church was open; it happened, as we say, to be choir practice night, and the Church was open just that one night in the week between seven and eight. This was the more remarkable, for though Mr Bligh Bond had written to us both that the meeting was at 8 p.m. he had intended to say 8.30 and gave that hour to Mrs Hester Dowden, who did not get home from dining out till that hour and was surprised to find us waiting. Had Mr Bligh Bond put 8.30 on our letters we should certainly not have arrived in Chelsea till after 8 p.m. and then the church would, no doubt, have been closed.

Of course it may have been a pure accident, but those who have read this story from the beginning will, I think, feel more inclined to say that it was all part of an angel directed and divinely ordered plan.

The Vicar was in his cassock and the organist was taking the practice. The Vicar seeing us enter came down the nave to meet us and I asked him might we see the place in which the Tudor royal personages, and especially the Princess Elizabeth, used to worship.

He was very kind and wanted to show us all kinds of other interesting things as well, but I told him that we had only a quarter of an hour to spare and only wanted to see the old royal chapel. He then showed us where it was. I then asked him might

we have the light turned down a little in that part as we wished
to kneel in prayer. He very kindly did this and so we found ourselves in the very spot where many a time had knelt the Lady
Anne and Elizabeth and Sir Thomas Moore, and above all the
very man whom we were called to help: strange indeed if this
was purely accidental.

As we knelt the choir sang most exquisitely the hundred-and-
twenty-first Psalm which will evermore be connected in my mind
with that spot and hour. It was the very message I was needing,
the promise of protection from the evil powers which we were
about to grapple with, and I am persuaded that we were called
into that Church not so much to pray as to be assured of Divine
protection.

I rose from my knees fearless and all nervousness and anxiety
passed away. Rightly or wrongly it came as a direct message
from God to me that He was giving His angels charge concerning
me, and that my task had been divinely appointed.

(On my return home the next day Maud asked me if I did
not feel afraid of entering such a conflict with evil, and I could
truly say, 'No, I felt absolutely no fear, nothing but a great sense
of pity for Henry seemed to take possession of me'. And it was I
believe this sense of and filling of my heart with pity and desire
to help him that at last made an impression when all seemed to
have proved fruitless.)

We then went to the house, and were shown into a large upstairs drawing-room with a grand piano, and had to wait half
an hour as Mr Bligh Bond had made this mistake in the time.

At 8.30 Mrs Hester Dowden came in dressed in evening dress,
with Mr Bligh Bond, and apologised for keeping us waiting and
said she had all along been told 8.30 and Mr Bligh Bond could
not understand how he had written 8 o'clock to both of us, as
he had fixed 8.30 from the beginning. However, we told her
that she need not apologise as the mistake had given us the
privilege of seeing the old church.

H.D. 'I am afraid I do not yet know who I am speaking to, I
only know you are Mr Bligh Bond's friends and have not
heard your names.'

Then Miss Kelly explained that it was most important that she should not know anything about us or the purpose of our visit until after the meeting if she did not mind, and to this she laughingly consented.

'I think I might tell you,' said Miss Kelly, 'that our meeting tonight is the result of a message which was sent to us over a year ago; my friend and Mr Bligh Bond and myself were asked to meet, with someone quite in ignorance of the purpose for which we were called together, but we were told that a certain work was to be done through the co-operation of the seen and unseen worlds and that without our help it could not be effected. We have been unable to meet sooner as we live in different parts of England and tonight is our first opportunity.'

The drawing-room was well lighted with electric light and there were two ladies and another gentleman present besides ourselves.

Mrs Hester Dowden as she was speaking to us heard the name Katherine, Katherine, Katherine, repeated three times, whether it was someone named Katherine who was calling or whether it was someone calling for Katherine she could not say, but she at once sat down at a table with a pencil in her hand and the following was written.

'Johannes (Hester Dowden's guide) is here and I am sending someone to speak. It is a person who says she has been in this neighbourhood often.'

There was a pause and then was written—

'My name is Katherine. I want to explain to you why I have come here. I know you are a person who is quite outside any interest in us. But I am interested in this place where you live because almost on the spot of ground beneath this house many curious events took place in bygone times.'

Here Mrs Hester Dowden interrupted, saying, 'I assure you you are wrong.'

Katherine taking no notice—'In the time which interests me this place you live in was a garden and people walked here who were of importance. I want you to help someone who needs help from your world.'

H.D.   'Please explain, I haven't the faintest idea of what you are talking about.'

Johannes. 'It is because of something that makes her suffer. She wants you to help her, if you can help to find out certain matters for her she will be happier here. I have been sent here tonight as a messenger from her.'

H.D. 'But she really must be clearer.'

P.W. 'No, it is all right, let her go in her own way. We know who it is and she is leading up to what we want.'

Though I was utterly unprepared for it, I knew at once that it was Katherine of Aragon.

H.D. 'Well, I'm glad you understand her for I'm sure I don't know what she's driving at.'

We were asked to draw our chairs nearer to the table.

Katherine. 'Now I feel great strength and I think there is a real help here. I want you to make this woman (Mrs H.D.) do all she can for she seems to me to have a very clear brain and can contain that which is needful. You seem to me to have found a right person. Ask her to help you.'

H.D. 'I will do what I can.'

K. 'I want to tell you that there is a place near this house where contact can be very much clearer. In fact it would be almost certain to bring the actual person who needs help so sorely.'

J. 'I will give you all the information I can. If you will look at those houses near the river close by where you are, you will see a garden between them and that is the very spot which she wants you to visit to make the contact close.'

H.D. 'I don't know of any such place, you must try to explain it a little more exactly.'

J. 'If you pass by the right of this house along the river bank you will come to two houses rather far apart. The garden is between them.'

B.B. 'How does it lie with regard to the Church?'

J. 'It is before you come to the Church.'

H.D.	'I don't know of any such place; would it help if we went there tonight?'
J.	'Yes, of course it would, you will be standing in the very grounds.'
H.D.	'Which of us should go?'
J.	'You and the gentleman beside you (myself) must go.'

This was indeed exciting. We got out hats and coats, and Mrs H.D., myself and Miss Kelly left the house, Mrs H.D. taking a pencil and a paper block in her hand. We followed the directions carefully down to the river, then along the river bank across the entrance to a big street and as we were nearing the Church where we had so lately knelt in prayer, I saw two houses apart with a field or open space between them, with a tall close wooden palisade shutting the field from the view of the road.

P.W. 'I expect this is the place, let us stop and ask.'
H.D. 'Are we at the right spot?' Aloud.
'Yes, yes,' was written on the block.
'I want you to stand here and ask for him.' (This was probably written by Katherine.)

There were three or four steps up to the door beside the palisade; we went up them so as to be able to look into the field and then Miss Kelly said softly but clearly.

'Henry, can you hear us. Are you here?'

At once the pencil wrote violently, 'I am here, Henry Rex.'

It was rather dark and the Henry Rex was not quite plain, so I said, 'please write your name again'.

This time there could be no mistake and in bold letters and a dash which tore the paper was written again – HENRY REX.

Then Miss Kelly said: 'Henry will you come back with us to the house?'

In strong bold letters was written: 'Yes, I will come'.

We stood for a moment reading the writing under the lamp, and then as we had evidently accomplished our purpose we returned to the house where the others were waiting for us. We had not been away more than a quarter of an hour.

We sat down again and at once Mrs Hester Dowden's hand wrote: 'Katherine is here. I want you to help him. He is in this room now. Will you speak to him? He is only recovering from the shock.'

For some reason or other Katherine's presence must have been unknown to him, just as it was unseen to us.

E.K.	'Henry, we are here to help you if we can.'
Reply.	'Henry Rex.'
B.B.	'Do you realise that you have died?'
H.Rex.	'Yes, I know. It has been but a nightmare.'
E.K.	'It need not be, if you take the help that is ready to be given to you.'
H.R.	'Who can help a King?'
B.B.	'You are a King no longer.'
H.R.	'I am a King. I carry my royal birth and death in my hands.'
B.B.	'Can you not realize that death levels us all?'
H.R.	'I have slept for a long time. This awakening seems more painful than sleep. Yes, I know this is one of those people they have sent.'
P.W.	'We want to help you Henry.'
H.R.	'I want to be told exactly what has happened and why I am still in a dark place I feel as if I was back again in the earth.'
B.B.	'You *are* back among people on the earth.'
H.R.	'In that garden I walked.'
B.B.	'Yes, centuries ago. You remember what the Church taught about purgatory.'
H.R.	'Yes, that was fire. I have been sleeping.'
B.B.	'Purgatory is not all fire.'
H.R.	'Yes, so the Church told us. I shall have my trial in the fires.'
B.B.	'Not external fires but fires of the soul.'
H.R.	'I know better. It will be fire which will scorch out my sins.'
E.K.	'Can you not remember any of the harm you did?'
H.R.	'What harm did I do? I only executed the rights of a King.'
B.B.	'You acted cruelly to your wives and executed some of them.'

H.R. 'They had a time. I had a right to do what came to me from my divine Kingship.'

B.B. 'What about the Abbot of Glastonbury whom you hanged, what do you think of that now?'

H.R. 'What do I think now? I have not thought for centuries. I want to walk in the garden again.'

B.B. 'Have you not just been walking there?'

H.R. 'No, I do not remember.'

P.W. 'Henry do you remember Elizabeth?'

H.R. 'I do. She was nothing to me.'

B.B. 'She became a great Queen of England and we are all very proud of her.'

H.R. 'I did not expect it from her Mother's child.'

P.W. 'Did you not judge her wrongly?'

H.R. 'Can you believe that any man misjudges. He merely passes from one mood to another. Who can control the mind?'

P.W. 'Yes, Henry, God can control the mind, and He can call men to account for these things.'

H.R. 'I will tell you what God does with me. I don't know where or what tortures I am going to. I believe in the Church.'

B.B. 'It's strange to hear you say that you believe in the Church.'

H.R. 'Why should I not believe in the Church?'

(I felt that time was passing and that we were making no impression and lifting up my heart in prayer for guidance I determined once more to appeal to him through the Lady Anne's death.)

P.W. 'Henry, you condemned Elizabeth's mother. She was an innocent woman and you knew it.'

H.R. 'That was unfair. But I reserve the privilege of considering her guilty.'

P.W. 'Can you not feel pity for her and be sorry?'

H.R. '*My* time for pity has come if I am to be awakened to these reproaches. I am not sorry. A King does not commit acts for which he is sorry. I shall be able to endure my trial. I am prepared for that if it means fire.'

P.W.   'The Divine right of Kings will not be recognised.'

H.R.   'I shall not listen to *you*. You are a fool. I would have had you executed in my time. Do you know that England's reigning King is present with you tonight. A look from me would have withered you up; if I had only eyes I could make you feel.'

B.B.   'Can you realise that King George V is our sovereign now?'

H.R.   'I care not. You are a varlet; some knave from a tavern, who is making sport of me because I lie at your mercy.'

(I felt that in this mood we could never reach him and made one more effort to appeal to him through his better feelings.)

P.W.   'Henry, you admit you were unfair to Anne, yet she bears you no ill will.'

H.R.   'Where is Anne? I seem to feel her near me.'

E.K.   'Look for her; she is not far off.'

(Evidently the Lady Anne was present and helping according to her promise.)

H.R.   'I laid my head on her lap when it ached and I sought her in my vexations. Then I threw her from me, as a poor fool does when he is alive and does not know the value of his friends. But she whined. How could a King bear with a puling, whey-faced creature who wept and wept.'

P.W.   'She is happy now and pities you from her heart and is willing to help you if you will let her.'

(I feel now that I might have done much better if I had approached him through Katherine who was the one really interested in him and evidently the one that night trying to reach him. But it is easy to be wise after the event. I was so unprepared for Katherine's advent and had so got it into my head that I could reach his better self through pity for Anne that I fear I did not do as well as I might have. After all, it was Katherine of Aragon who was the real true wife and as the Lady Anne had only that afternoon showed me her relationship to Henry was now a sealed book and had been but an unhappy episode in her life. I got what I deserved in the next reply.)

H.R.   'I shall be pleased to receive her homage again if she comes to me.'

P.W.   'It's more than homage, Henry. You need her pardon. Will you seek it?'

H.R.   'No, I make errors, but I do not recognise them. A King's privilege is to err, and not to be considered a sinner.'

B.B.   'Think of her as a woman and of yourself as a man. Can you not then find some pity for her?'

H.R.   'I will not listen to your foolish talk, I have been in darkness and hell has caught me in a shroud, which I can no more break than a bird from a snare, but I shall only recognise my Queen when she craves pardon of *me*, for a wanton rebellious spirit.'

P.W.   'There are others here tonight waiting to help you if only you will let them.'

H.R.   'You are one of those creatures (priests or monks) no doubt. Are you one of the Holy Church I deposed?'

P.W.   'Henry, I am a clergyman, but I cannot help you without your co-operation. Don't lose the opportunity.'

H.R.   'You convey to me the sense that I can find pardon for my sins and escape punishment by prayer.'

P.W.   'Yes, if you begin with prayer and penitence the whole road is open before you to final happiness.'

H.R.   'I will pray, for there is nothing to be lost in dignity for any man who prays, but I only preserve my poor mind in this sorry place by remembering I am a King and will be England's King when I meet my punishment.'

P.W.   'You cannot escape punishment, but punishment when accepted in the right spirit is a discipline and will do you good.'

B.B.   'If you are indeed a King, then bear it like a King.'

P.W.   'Henry, this is God's way for you, penitence and prayer. Will you pray?'

H.R.   'I will, Holy Father, pray, but tell this varlet he deserves a whipping and would have it bestowed on him right generously if I lived. I cannot.'

P.W.   'He is not a varlet. He is not a clergyman, but he wants to help you as we all do.'

(Then as I saw that an impression had at last been produced, I made one more strong appeal.)

P.W.   'Henry, begin now at once to pray and ask the Lord Jesus to help you.'

H.R.   'I will make my orisons away from here. I will not pray here. A King prays alone.'

And with this promise the pencil ceased writing and this strange interview came to an end.

Have we done any good was my first thought. Have we done what was wanted or have we failed. Perhaps we should have begun from Katherine and the wrong done to her.

'No, I don't think so,' said Mr Bligh Bond, 'I think it was all right, but let us see if we can get information. To get him to promise to pray is a great step and perhaps we can find out if it has had any result.'

So Mrs Hester Dowden again took the pencil and it wrote:

'Johannes is here. I have your question on my mind. I heard you ask whether you could help this great King who sinned. I cannot explain what has happened to him, unless I go back very far into history, but he says what is quite true when he stated that he has been asleep all this time. It is also true that the desire of a woman who has pinned her faith on this man has called him from his state of lethargy; now he will pass on and come to one of the spheres where there will be time for meditation and growth. You cannot do much for him personally, but you can keep touch with the woman and help her to get borne away from that desire that eats away her soul. Speak to her and help her. The King will come out of this unhappy state in which he is at present in time – a time that to you would seem long. You need not pity him, but pity her for she is troubled by her love of this man even now when she has passed over here so long. Help her by telling her that she has helped him by her suffering and that she will help him more by forgetting her misery, for misery creates misery and her unhappiness keeps him back.

Johannes.'

E.K. 'Is Katherine there?'

J.   'Yes, she is waiting. Katherine is speaking. Kate is with the King.'

Evidently our work had succeeded in what was probably its main purpose, though that purpose was unknown to us, to enable Katherine to reach Henry.

E.K.   'Katherine you must not trouble so much for him, your grief injures him, and you will help him most by trying to forget your own misery.'

K.   'I am happy now that I have set him free. I shall help him, but you must pray for us both, good people. I shall be here many a time again to tell this tale to the hand that is holding the pen. I want you to receive all that can come from the thanks that a poor woman can give you. I am only perfect when my master and king is near.

I will obey though it gives me pain. But what do you ask if you ask forgetfulness; it cannot come.

Good people, pray for me and my King for we need help. He has many a sore trial before him. When you pray think of me in the garden near the river for I have had much of joy and suffering there.'

With this message of gratitude from Katherine this memorable meeting closed.

Her entrance upon the scene had been so utterly unexpected, and the attitude of Henry so different from what I had imagined it would be, should we reach him, that it made it difficult to adjust oneself to the conditions as they actually were and I was afraid at first that we had failed our unseen friends and fellow workers. But this message of Katherine made it evident that a great deal had been accomplished, and probably the very results had been obtained for which we had been called together in such a strange way.

Henry had evidently been aroused and as Katherine put it 'set free', probably by his being persuaded to leave the garden. He had also promised to pray which he felt he could do without losing his dignity; and finally the faithful long-suffering Katherine had reached him and would now help him through his trials.

I am writing up this part of the story in my quiet study in my 'Tudor Corner' on January 28th, just ten days after it all took place, and though it sounds so amazing and incredible it seemed very real and natural that night, and at the Holy Communion service last Sunday in my little Church with its beautiful Tudor doorway, two fresh names were, I confess, upon my lips in prayer, Henry and Katherine.

CHAPTER ELEVEN

MORE COINCIDENCES

Spiritual realities do not in the last instance admit of proof, in a mathematical or scientific sense, and a friend is right in saying that there is no absolute proof for any spiritual phenomenon. I admire his logical consistency which not only refuses to believe all modern spiritual phenomena, but all spiritual phenomena whatsoever, including all the miracles of the Old and New Testaments with the Transfiguration and Resurrection of our Lord and of course such stories as the release of St Peter from prison.

They cannot be absolutely proved and therefore they cannot be credited, such a position is strictly speaking logical and understandable. But to say as so many professing Christians do that they believe that there have been in Bible times, and in Church history times spiritual phenomena, but that they are impossible now, has really nothing to commend it and is quite illogical.

This whole story, remarkable and even amazing as I admit it to be, all hangs together in a very wonderful way and it seems to me more difficult to put it all down to accident or self-deception than to take it as an extraordinary but Divinely planned and allowed working out of the 'Communion of Saints' in which we profess to believe.

And now to pass to some more curious coincidences which, though they do not actually prove the story true, still certainly are very remarkable and seem more than merely accidental.

When I left Chelsea at 11 p.m. I got a bus to Stamford Brook as I was staying the night with my friend, Rev. H. Brierley Thomson at St Mary's Vicarage.

I found him up and waiting for me and when I told him what had taken place he said, 'Well, I am extremely interested for I was a curate in Chelsea for many years and know every inch of it. Tell me exactly where the garden was.' So I described the spot. 'I know it well,' he said, 'why, all that part was the old Tudor Manor House grounds. I will get the map of Chelsea and show it to you.'

So the map was got of Chelsea in the Tudor times and then, to my astonishment, I saw that what Katherine had just said and which Mrs Hester Dowden had denied, was absolutely correct. The house of Mrs Hester Dowden was standing on probably the very site of the old Tudor Manor House, where Katherine had lived herself.

Then we found the actual spot where we had found Henry and to which we had been directed, and it was another garden which adjoined the Manor House grounds and only yesterday I had a letter from Mrs Hester Dowden who writes in amazement: 'Last Sunday a lady who knows Chelsea very well was here, and told me that the garden we were directed to was the ground upon which Henry VIII's hunting lodge was built. The lodge is in Glebe Place, a good way from the Embankment.'

So that, unknown to ourselves, we were guided to this very spot to which Henry was no doubt specially attached.

In a court of law I venture to think this would be regarded as strong corroborative evidence, though not reaching actual proof.

It was strange too coming to stay that night with a man who, as he said, knew every inch of Chelsea, and could at once place the map and information before me. Perhaps a pure coincidence, but perhaps part of a wonderfully well-planned-out guidance.

And now for another striking coincidence. Hester Dowden did not, of course even know my name, nor did I know anything about her. But when I got back to my parish I wrote to thank her for her kindness and sent her a copy of my play and also Part I of my story to read.

She replied:

Dear Mr Pakenham-Walsh,

Thank you very much indeed for your play, which I look forward to reading with great pleasure . . . .

I hope when you are in town again you will ring me up.

I remember a Mr Herbert Pakenham-Walsh visiting my father often on Sundays. You may have known him also; Prof. E. Dowden.

With kind regards and many thanks –

Sincerely yours,

Hester Dowden.

How extraordinary! I am sent to a complete stranger and she turns out to be the daughter of my brother's great friend and former tutor in Trinity College, Dublin, and known, of course, though less intimately, by me also, and this complete stranger also lives on the very one spot in England where it was probably essential that we should meet.

But a third coincidence was yet to come. Mr Thomson had just secured a new housekeeper. She was a clergyman's daughter but in the great distress of the times was obliged to seek a livelihood.

She was a bright, intelligent looking woman of about thirty-six, and was also possessed of some psychic gifts, and among them something of which I had no experience whatever, namely, crystal reading, and Mr Thomson suggested that before I left next day, we should ask her to read the crystal and see if she could at all tell anything about my story of which, of course, she knew absolutely nothing.

CHAPTER TWELVE

THE CRYSTAL

I had never seen a crystal, so after breakfast next day, Saturday, January 19th, Mr Thomson showed it to me. It looks just
like a round ball of glass about twice the size of a billiard ball.
Mr Thomson put it on a black velvet cloth and asked me to
look into it. I did so and saw two faces, a small face, my own
in front; and a big face, my own again upside down behind.

I looked till I was tired, but nothing more interesting ap-
pearing, I felt inclined to chuck the ball out of the window.

'Would you like Miss E. to come and try,' said Mr
Thomson.

'Yes,' I said, 'but it seems to me a rather hopeless kind of
concern.'

So Miss E. was called in. She asked me to hold the crystal
ball in my hand and if I wished to see anything special to
think of it.

I said to myself, I wish the Lady Anne would, if she can,
show some pictures which would go to confirm that our work
last night was a reality and that it had been successful.

I handed back the ball. Miss E. put it on the black velvet
cloth.

Then Mr Thomson asked me had I anything of the Lady
Anne's I could give Miss E.

'No,' I said, 'of course not; the only things belonging to her
are in Hever Castle.'

'Well, I should get the paper with Henry Rex written on
it and give it, as if it is genuine, it will belong to the period.'

So I got the paper and it was folded and Miss E. put it
against her forehead and then shading her eyes looked into the
crystal.

And then after a pause of perhaps three minutes came this extraordinary series of pictures, which I personally could never have thought of, and the full meaning of which I hardly fully grasped at the time.

PICTURE I

I see a woman's face, rather oval and pale. She has some kind of band across her forehead, it might possibly be a nun and yet she is not like a nun. She has brown hair and brown hazel eyes.

She is standing by a tree and looking at a window. The window is rather square with a kind of rounded top; it is not a modern building, but is built of grey stone and above the window are what seem like narrow windows or openings.

Now I see a round pool of water; there is a red glow behind the window, which might be the sun setting.

*   *   *

Of course, it was the Lady Anne; the band is across her forehead in all her pictures; the face is oval and pale and the hair and eyes brown.

The window is her bedroom in Hever Castle and the narrow openings are the battlements above it.

The round pool of water, I must try and find out, as I cannot remember if it was round, and anyway the shape may have altered, but it is most probably the moat under the window.

But what is most remarkable is that looking at her window, she would be looking West and so the sun would be setting behind it.

It may be said that Miss E. was reading my mind. But such a picture or idea was not in my mind at all, nor ever had been. I was thinking then of Chelsea and rather expecting a picture of the old Tudor House there.

PICTURE II

Now I see a man's face. It is squarish with a short beard. I cannot see the whole face but it looks a rough face. There seems something strange on the head, some kind of flat hat, possibly a college cap.

*   *   *

Those who know Henry's pictures need not be told who this was.

PICTURE III

Now I see the same man alone in a chapel praying. His back is to me; he has a stout heavy figure, I cannot see his face, but it is the same man and he is praying alone.

*   *   *

It will be remembered that Henry's parting words were 'A King prays alone'.

Evidently the two pictures were to mark the contrast, the rough-faced man and the man praying alone, meaning, I take it, that a great change had taken place, and that our work of the night before had not been in vain.

We met him a rough-faced man. We left him a man alone in prayer. All this, so effective, was quite beyond my imagination.

PICTURE IV

Now I see the woman's face again. She is looking through a window. The window seems barred in some way, bars as in squares. It is the same woman, but she seems very sad and pale and all round her is a blue light, it is the halo of devotion.

*   *   *

The Tower of London and 'The little sad room of many memories' in which I had once stood and the barred window overlooking Tower Hill, out of which I too had once looked.

The pale face looking out of the barred window and around her the halo of devotion as she made ready for the cruel end, and asked on that last night might she receive the sacred emblems and once again attest her innocence.

A perfect, yet pathetic picture, but quite beyond me to have drawn in those few lines.

PICTURE V

Now I see a pillar, it looks like a stone pillar and now there is a man with some kind of dark thing over his face. I cannot see it very clearly as it seems to be in a gloomy court-yard. There are windows all round and it seems such a dark gloomy place.

Now there is what looks like a crescent beside the man, it looks very bright and stands out very clearly against the gloom.

*   *   *

'Yes,' I said, 'I know too well what the picture means. Now can the woman bring herself into that picture and it will be absolutely complete. She should be in the picture to complete it and there is only one attitude in which she can appear in it.'

There was a pause of a few seconds.

PICTURE VI

Now I see a woman. It is the same woman, but I can only see her profile. She seems dressed in some long clinging robe. Now she is bending forward in rather a curious attitude. She looks very slight, frail in figure.

*   *   *

How this Miss E. drew this picture, I don't pretend to explain; but of course it was too perfect. The pillar was the block passed on the way in the Tower Green: the French executioner with his masked face, the gleaming crescent sword which was used that day instead of the axe: the gloomy court-yard surrounded with windows, and then the slight frail woman's figure bending forward, not resting her head on a block, is all absolutely and vividly correct.

PICTURE VII

Now I seem to see the woman's head above her. The woman has disappeared and there is the figure of her head alone.

It is the figure of her head, but it looks very frigid like marble. It is still beautiful but like a statue, the neck is very graceful, what one would call a swan-like neck.

But there seems no life or colour about it; and it might almost be the head of a dead woman.

*   *   *

I leave it at that. I cannot explain it. I can only say once again that Miss E. knew absolutely nothing about me or my story and that, on my part, such a set of pictures was neither in my mind nor power to produce. If the Lady Anne heard my wish and gave them herself to assure me that our work for Henry had not been either in vain or an unreality then there is a reason for them, and they are at least explainable, but on no other supposition can I see any cause for them or such a series of vivid and true pictures could have been produced.

CHAPTER THIRTEEN

HOME SWEET HOME

Shortly after the meeting at Chelsea we invited Miss Kelly on a visit to our home at Sulgrave, and she asked whether it was desired that she should go and she received the following message:—

> January 28th, 1924. Yes, it is indeed desired that you should go to visit the Irish priest and his sweet wife. We here have work in hand for him to do in due time. He needs enlightenment in many things relating to our condition here in this world called by you the next, but in very truth it is no more next than your own, as though one should say on retiring from one room in a dwelling to another, I go into the next house. Not so, my sister, we go upstairs if you like, some of us, where our windows reveal a wider view than in the basements, but it is one "house", this wherein we dwell, both thou and I, a house of many rooms. Yes, very many, but one roof over all, one Master of the building, one home for His great family. Seek truth and reveal it; be patient, gentle, wise; wait on the Lord for His commands and obey without question when thou hast received His bidding; take courage be of confident good cheer, thy work will come, prepare thyself for thy well doing. God bless thee.

A few days later came another communication, this time telling something of what had really been effected at Chelsea.

> Alwyn the Saxon Thane sends to thee greeting, would have thee know much of help has resulted from the meeting held to rouse Henry. The love of one woman has availed greatly but she who came to ask thine aid will still need it. Do thou and the brothers pray for her, that strength to endure may be given her to overcome the sloth of soul in this the man she truly loves.
>
> And pray ye all for one another. See that ye keep pure in heart, seeking the Lord thy God in all things. Then indeed may earth's messengers be given trust to receive and tell out again

the teaching of the Word to men. God ever bless and guide thy steps upon His holy paths of love.

One of the company of Avilon.

Miss Kelly came to us on Saturday, February 9th, from Brighton and it was a delightful visit, as she was able to tell such wonderful stories of the help she had been led to give both to those living and to those whom we call dead. She will probably some day publish her experiences.

On February 12th, as we were sitting over the fire, there came the following message through her hand:—

'God bless this house and all the work to be done from it. Cast fear out of your heart. Trust prayer and faith as the guide. I who speak come on behalf of a soul for whose deliverance your aid has been required. Great results are not to be looked for at first, but little by little God's light begins to pierce the darkness in his soul.'

Here Miss Kelly said the vibrations altered and the Lady Anne took up the message.

'Anne says make no forced opportunity, but be assured she will be ready to perform her share in cleansing that page of the book I closed, blinded to the truth since borne in upon my spirit that for such share as was mine I must make my reparation too with his. Elizabeth our daughter has gone to seek for her father, she too has much to redeem. Cross over and behold this night the power of love. All can meet who work in unison. Sleep in your awakening, we meet you in a place set apart for this very purpose. (None of us had any dream that night that we could remember.) Join hands as you sit, now.'

We three joined hands as directed.

P.W. 'Is it the Lady Anne who is speaking?'

Anne. 'Yes, join hands and wait.'

E.K. 'I see a Tudor rose. Under the rose is a fire. It is symbolic of purification. Now behind the rose I see Henry and Anne and between them and drawing them both together is Elizabeth. Behind them now I see a number of shadowy figures and in the distance a crucifix.'

This completed the very symbolic picture and we unjoined hands.

Anne. 'Wait now and be ready if again we ask you to help us. Say to these parents their child is very near them always.

It makes her happy to be one of them; not left out as so many are. Be kind to all strangers brought for enlightenment as many will be ere long, I mean souls from our side. Men from this village throng about you where you meet their people: try to realise their presence and then you can make it known to others.'

Here the Lady Anne ceased to speak, and though what follows is not directly connected with the present story it is so very beautiful and helpful that I shall include it in this chapter.

'Dear father and my own darling mother, I your little daughter Helen am here standing so close to you. I wish, oh how I wish, you could see me as clearly as I see you. I do see you better tonight than I ever have. I see even your clothing and all the things lying about on the tables and chairs. I have never seen like this before, why is it I can. Well, please, I like it, only I wish all the others were here too (her four brothers at school). I can get nearest to Harold. I often go and see him.'

Her mother. 'Where do you go to see him?'

Helen. 'In school and anywhere.'

Mother. 'How old is Harold, can you remember?'

Helen. 'No. Did I come first?'

Mother. 'Yes, you left us in March and he came in April next year.'

Helen. 'I don't know about March and April. Who are they?'

Father. 'Do you know Lilian?'

Helen. 'Oh, yes.'

Father. 'She is asleep now, upstairs.'

Helen. 'I will just pop up and kiss her. . . . It didn't take me long. Mother, what a darling my sister is; would I have grown up big like that?'

Mother. 'Yes, much bigger.'

Helen. 'Was I big for my age, I mean?'

Mother. 'You were only three months old, so of course you were small.'

Helen.	'But can't a baby be big for its age at three months?'
Mother.	(Laughing.) 'You were just a beautiful dear little baby.'
Helen.	'Well, as you are my father and mother, may I tell you what I am like now?'
Mother.	'Yes, please.'
Helen.	'I am fairly tall people say, and my hair is goldy brown and my eyes are grey.'
Father.	'What are you doing Helen?'
Helen.	'I am still more or less at school.'
Father.	'Who teaches you?'
Helen.	'Oh! lots of glorious teachers, but I learn my A.B.C. sometimes with Lilian. I mean I have to learn to understand your kind of lessons.'
Mother.	'Did you learn with Harold?'
Helen.	'No, I seem to remember so little till not long ago.'
Mother.	'Can you remember another brother's name?'
Helen.	'Same name as Daddy.' (William.)
Father.	'Do you know the Lady Anne?'
Helen.	'Oh, yes.'
Mother.	'Do you know your other brother's names?'
Helen.	'Herbert and Eric.'
Mother.	'Do you know Granny?'
Helen.	'Which Granny?'
Mother.	'Your mother's mother.'
Helen.	'Yes, I love her very much, she takes charge of me sometimes.'
Mother.	'Do you know your Daddy's mother.'
Helen.	'Yes, I see her, but I don't live with her. Mother's own granny is often making plans to help you all.'
Mother.	'Which Granny?'
Helen.	'I mean your mother's mother. Now I have to go, mother dear and my daddy. Daddy, I come too and listen when you preach.'
Father.	'We think of you as if you were here with us.'
Helen.	'I always am. I mean I come a lot, but I have work as well as lessons and play. I am learning to help children here.'

Father.	'Shall we ever be able to see you?'
Helen.	'I don't know, Daddy, but I'll ask, but can you see?'
Father.	'No.'
Helen.	'Perhaps you will.'
Father.	'Did the Lady Anne ever bring you before?'
Helen.	'Yes, more than once, and Lois is my friend, one I've made just lately. She is much older than I am.'
Mother.	'Do you know who she is?'
Helen.	'No, it doesn't matter. She says she lived a long time ago but that does not mean she is old.'
Mother.	'Helen, do you know what my mother does?'
Helen.	'Granny is a ministering spirit for those in ignorance and sin; like all people who serve she works to rescue.'
Mother.	'It's quite time you went to bed (11.15 p.m.). Kiss me goodnight.'
Father.	'Do try and come to us direct.'
Helen.	'Yes, Daddy, I do try.'
Father.	'Can we help you?'
Helen.	'Try now and feel when I kiss you goodnight . . . . there did I kiss you Daddy?'
Father.	'I'm sure I don't know.'
Helen.	'Mother did you feel me? I've kissed you both, but I'll try again. I'm going now.' (Waving her hand.)

How the threads of life are interwoven and overlap between the seen and the unseen. Here is Lois, who was evidently a girl of the Tudor period, making friends with Helen because she is my child and so there is a link between them. All these relationships seem so delicate and sympathetic and yet so natural and if we can make friends as our Lord says with the Mammon of unrighteousness how much more through our deeper interests, friends also doubtless on the other side of the veil who shall receive us into the everlasting habitation. How such a thought deepens and beautifies all life, even in the humblest spheres, at least that is the impression the friendship of Lois and Helen produced in my mind, and I think it is well worth introducing into the story.

CHAPTER FOURTEEN

KATHERINE OF ARAGON'S SHRINE

In June 1924, I was attending a conference at Peterborough and was the guest of Mrs Clayton, the widow of a former Suffragan Bishop of the diocese.

She of course knew nothing of my interest in the Tudor period, but she told me a very interesting story connected with the tomb of Queen Katherine whose body had been laid to rest in the Cathedral.

The stone over the vault had fallen into disrepair and the name Katherine had become almost obliterated when the idea occurred to Mrs Clayton that as her name was Katherine she would make an appeal to all the Katherines in England for subscriptions to have a handsome marble slab laid down to take the place of the old one.

The appeal was successful and when the Spanish Ambassador heard the story from Mrs Clayton he was so pleased with the kind way in which the Queen was still remembered in England that he made the story known in Spain and just before my visit, Mrs Clayton had had a letter from a Madrid Historical Association thanking her and all her fellow Katherines for their kindness and thoughtfulness in caring for the tomb of the Spanish Princess.

It is said that the Abbey at Peterborough was spared the fate of Glastonbury, Fountains and other Abbeys because when the King was asked if he was not going to build a Monument to his first wife he replied, 'She shall have the finest Monument in England, Peterborough Cathedral shall be her Shrine', and so the Abbey became a Cathedral.

With my special interest in the Tudor period I felt it a double honour when on November 25th, 1953, I was made a Canon of Peterborough Cathedral by my beloved Bishop Leeson, whose home call in 1956 aged only sixty-one, was such a great loss to the whole Church. He was one of the first to become a Vice-President of the Churches' Fellowship for Psychical Study and to him the movement owes a great deal.

Before I left I knelt at Katherine's tomb and after I had told
Eleanor Kelly of my experiences she had the following message
from Katherine herself.

Katherine. 'Listen sister whilst I speak–not Anne–Katherine.
I am grateful to all who offer prayer and help in
thoughts of kindness and of pity for my King: no
King in splendour but still King of my heart. I
who loved him as husband and father of my child,
as also did one other of his earthly wives. Anne loved
him in part I know, and loved him as father of
Elizabeth, but not so as I loved him and still retain
that love. Mine is he, mine he always was and mine
he will yet acknowledge himself to be; mine and I his
in the bond of peace and in righteousness of living at
last I hope and pray, and in my soul I know it will
be so. God leaves no soul to drift uncared for and
sends His many angels to direct and succour even
such as he, poor lost one as he seemed to be.

Thy voice calling him for me broke in upon his
empty ear, and he woke to faint remembrance of the
garden and of me who often walked with him there in
the early years of our wedded life, or ever he sought
to thrust a sword into my heart and sever it in twain
–poor bleeding heart of woman. Sister we suffer,
we of our sex, but I would not stay the suffering till
the bitter lessons of it are learned.

Anne is beside me as I write and sends her greet-
ings to thee and to that one she hath charge of in
his earthly pilgrimage. There is no sorrow or anger
between us any more; I grow in love of her and we
are one in our work of rescue.

Each had pride and sins of ambition to let fall and
to be cleansed from and in the baptism of the Spirit
we have washed and are made clean. Cease now as
thou canst catch no more with ease. We come again,
we and others; our niece Jane too.

Adieu Sister,

Katherine.'

If Miss Kelly is impersonating these different characters she must surely be a consumate artist, but she is far too good and sincere a woman to do so, even if she possessed such amazing ability.

But who would ever think of putting into Katherine's mouth the admission that 'Anne loved him' even though it is qualified by the words 'in part'.

I am always open to reason and suggestion, but I can see no explanation of this message except the simplest one, namely that it came from Katherine herself, and if the simplest one is the true one, then what a beautiful and natural picture is opened to us of a life where old misunderstandings and rivalries are forgotten and forgiven, and those who were at enmity on earth are joined together in harmony and love and can unitedly work for the salvation of one who had done them both such grevious injury.

It all seems to ring true and to be what we really expect and believe in our best moments and probably many who read this will say that they have learned nothing new.

But whether new or old, I give the message just as it came to Miss Kelly, and I confess it seems to me a picture of great hope and beauty.

LADY JANE GREY

I had long expected the Lady Jane Grey to become reconciled with the Lady Anne and Queen Katherine, and when she at last appeared on the scene she came on an errand which both surprised and interested me on personal grounds. In this first announcement she came as one primarily interested in my own child Lilian, aged at this time nine and a half. I include this interlude in my Tudor story as I believe that it helps to prove that wherever the explanation for these events lies, it does not lie in the theory of subconscious self, or telepathy or the reading of mind.

The letter came from Miss Kelly:—

July 13th, 1924, 6 a.m.

Lady Anne.

Take up the pencil and write for me sister.

Anne and another, whose neck was as slender as mine to sever, in the same way, poor innocent one, in her was no sin

of ambition, no vain trappings of the mind, but a soul clear
as a child's, and but a child still when her spirit passed to
freedom – Jane Grey, Lady Jane Grey as you know her.

She comes with me today and will continue with me till a
task we have in hand is fulfilled, one of guardianship and
love. . . . . .

Here followed an accurate and sympathetic assessment of my
own young daughter's character. The message then went on to
its astounding conclusion—

Tell them (my wife and myself) that we (the Lady Anne,
Lady Jane Grey and Lois) offer them special assistance in the
training of the child. Will they accept it? And when difficulties
arise and they are perplexed how best to deal with the growing soul, will they call us to aid her?

My wife and I talked this over very carefully, and we both felt
that it was too serious a responsibility to take. The whole question
of Guardian Angelship is one about which we know so little.
I wrote a long letter to Miss Kelly setting forth the grave doubts
which beset our minds. In spite of an understanding and reassur-
ing answer from her I determined to wait until I should have
some opportunity of speaking directly with the Lady Anne about
it and explaining my difficulty and asking her whether she and
the Lady Jane Grey and Lois would not, if they saw the opportunity, help our little Lilian apart from any consent or appeal
from us.

Such an opportunity came unexpectedly on September 10th in
Bournemouth, and after I had explained my ideas to the Lady
Anne and asked her to help, as it were 'off her own bat' she replied simply but effectively: 'We are helping', and so there I let
the matter drop.

One thing seems quite clear from this correspondence, that
Miss Kelly is far from reading my mind, and that the messages
sent through her are not a reflex action from my own thoughts
and desires.

CHAPTER FIFTEEN

HENRY REX AND KATHERINE

On Tuesday, September 9th, I had a letter from my sister in Bournemouth saying that Mrs Andrews and Mrs Clegg were staying with her for a short visit, and could I possibly come down for a night or two.

I took the afternoon train next day to Bournemouth and I found Mrs Clegg and Mrs Andrews at my sister's and immediately after supper by the fire I began to relate something of my experience at Chelsea of which Mrs Clegg had not heard when suddenly Mrs Clegg said:

'There is a very powerful personage here now; he is very strongly built, very broad, with squarish face and a flat kind of cap on his head with a plume on one side. He says, 'Ha, Ha,' and seems very jocular. He says you have helped him and he wants your hand.' (Here Mrs Clegg seized my hand very firmly and shook it.)

I was completely taken by surprise. I had been expecting to meet the Lady Anne, and was in no way prepared for this encounter so I just said quietly: 'Henry have I helped you?'

Henry. 'Yes.'

P.W. 'Well I am glad. There are many others trying to help you especially Katherine.'

Mrs C. 'He knows it. He says "Percy".'

P.W. 'Yes Henry, what about Percy?'

Henry. 'I wronged him.'

P.W. 'How did you wrong him? Begin there and tell me, it may help you. God's word says "Confess your sins to one another that ye may be healed". Make your confession to me.' (Mrs Clegg here drew herself up as though imitating his expression of pride and unwillingness, with her

hands on her hips striking the characteristic attitude of
Henry.) 'Then Henry I will help you to remember. Percy
loved the Lady Anne Boleyn and they were betrothed
and you came in and forced him to give her up, thus
spoiling the happiness of two lives. Then you married
the Lady Anne yourself and in three years you got tired
of her and then you murdered her, and the very next day
you married another woman. Is there not anything to
be ashamed of or sorry for in all that?'

Henry. 'Part of me seems to be sorry and another part seems not
to care.'

P.W. 'Exactly! The better part of you is really sorry, but the
worse part holds it back. You must let your better part
assert itself and conquer this wretched selfish part. Do
you remember these words, "If we say that we have no
sin we deceive ourselves and the truth is not in us, but
if we confess our sins, He is faithful and just to forgive
us our sins and to cleanse us from all unrighteousness".'

Henry. 'I have been absolved from all that.'

P.W. 'Who absolved you? If God had absolved you, you
would not be in such a miserable and unhappy condition,
Henry, there are many now who want to help you, if you
will only respond. Katherine and the Lady Anne and
your daughter Elizabeth the great Queen and Lady Jane
Grey and others.'

Henry. 'They can go to hell for all I care.'

P.W. 'Henry, there is no good talking like that. That is the
bad part of your nature gaining the upper hand.'

Henry. 'I want you to help me.'

P.W. 'And I want to help you, but how can I help you if you
talk like that.'

Henry. 'Think the best you can of me and pray for me, but don't
remind me of my misdeeds, it hurts.'

P.W. 'I don't want to hurt you unless to hurt you is the means
to help you. We all need to be helped and I want to
help you, and I will do as you ask. I will try to think the
best of you and I will try to pray for you more.'

Henry. 'You have helped.' (He shook my hand firmly and
left.)

It was all so unexpected and unprepared for that I wondered again had I made the best use of my opportunity. Mrs Clegg was quite taken by surprise also for she had not read or heard of my meeting with Henry at Chelsea, so that I do not see how the experience can be accounted for by telepathy or on any such line.

I had been planning in the train what questions I would put to the Lady Anne and Mrs Clegg knew I would be expecting to meet Lady Anne, but no Lady Anne appeared and on the contrary came one who was not in either of our thoughts.

Now I began to realise why I had been called the 'Missionary spirit of our band on earth', which had seemed to be so strange and meaningless. My help on earth apparently was needed, as being himself earth bound he could see and hear me, while they in the brighter and higher spirit realms could not reach him directly. I am only putting this forward as a possible and probably true explanation. I don't pretend to understand why the human agent is needed at all, but there is no waste in God's economy of Grace and unless the human agent had been necessary, it surely would not have been employed.

Evidently a great struggle was going on in Henry's nature and he had advanced to this extent that he had admitted that he had wronged Percy and also he had asked for prayer for himself, and said that he desired to be helped.

How different was this to his attitude at Chelsea where a king could do no wrong, and where his wives had only got what they deserved.

TUDOR PERSONAGES

After Henry had gone Mrs Clegg described an ascetic looking figure in a priest's garment wearing a cross whom she took to have been a high dignitary in the Church of Rome, and who had suffered through Henry.

I asked if it were Bishop Fisher, and Mrs Clegg said it was. I remembered then that he was one of the characters in my play and that I spoke of him as one whose sterling qualities Englishmen would one day recognise.

It seems that he too is now helping Henry.

He also made it known that he had felt and appreciated the

sympathetic reference I had made to him in my play, albeit a
very brief reference. Oh, how careful we should be in all that we
say, even of the so-called dead!

There came next another priest who also indicated that he
had been cruelly treated by Henry. I believed this to have been
Friar Peyto, a friend of Bishop Fisher's, who preached before
Henry and the Lady Anne at Greenwich denouncing the marriage and comparing Henry to Ahab. Henry put him in the
Tower and tortured him. But I must emphasise that it was not
until I got home, and was able to look up the story, that I
realised who it was, and this must prove that Mrs Clegg could
not have been reading my mind. It must be that he came as a
friend of Bishop Fisher's, and was taking part in Henry's rescue.

Mrs Clegg then went on to describe someone who could only
have been Queen Katherine. On being asked if I had helped her
at all she replied 'Yes, yes, prayer, prayer, prayer'. She indicated that the work of redemption would have a successful
outcome. So many were working to that end, in both worlds,
and that 'All can co-operate in prayer'.

The next morning Mrs Clegg described six figures, and from
her detailed descriptions I feel that among them were the Lady
Anne, the Lady Jane Grey, Queen Katherine, and Elizabeth.
These all stood together, their hands were clasped in symbol of
being reunited in spirit and in love. United in their efforts to
redeem Henry's soul through their love.

I learnt later that the two other figures were those of Percy
and Kingston, also members of the band of rescuers. Percy is of
course the son of the Earl of Northumberland who was betrothed
to the Lady Anne. Kingston is that Governor of the Tower under
Henry, Sir William Kingston, who had much to do with the
Lady Anne.

Although, as far as I know, I have none of those psychic
powers which enable ultra-sensitive persons to see and hear
these spirit beings, after some fifteen years of observation and first
hand investigations, I have become absolutely convinced that
there are those among us who are endowed with such powers.
I fully realise that such gifts may be abused, and it is the abuse
of such gifts that the Holy Scripture inveighs against. But I am
equally persuaded that these gifts may be dedicated to God who

gave them, as was done by Samuel and Elijah in olden times, by Joan of Arc and St Theresa of Avila in medieval times and by some of the best and truest Christians whom I know in modern times. It has been my good fortune to meet some half dozen such women, and the outcome of my acquaintance with them has been this story, which to me at least is both wonderful and suggestive as to a future life, and a very practical possible 'Communion of Saints'.

Another result has been an ever deepening sense of one's own ignorance and unworth, and also of the tremendous possibilities open to humanity and to prayer.

So far from the knowledge of this angel ministry lessening one's sense of the greatness of the Christ, it seems to me to increase one's realisation of how great and loving He must be and how wonderful His Salvation.

CHAPTER SIXTEEN

PEACEHAVEN

AUGUST 1925

As we were staying at Hove, it was suggested that we should all go to see Miss Kelly in her little bungalow at Peacehaven bringing a tent to sleep in, and helping her with the cutting of her grass. Miss Kelly lived in a very very small and remote bungalow, but it was beautifully neat and so there seemed room for everything, and it looked out over the South Downs with their ever changing shades and moods, and down into the little village of Telscombe.

Miss Kelly gave us a warm welcome and before starting work we sat down to our lunch on the grass and pitched the tent. Then while the boys were working at making and trenching a flower bed, Miss Kelly took the opportunity of telling me that she had a message from the Lady Anne in which Willy (our eldest son) was mentioned. Just before coming to Hove, Maud and I felt that as Willy was now of age and was so frequently coming in contact with the modern psychic movement, and was studying philosophy, we should let him read this whole story so far as it had gone, and so be able to speak to him more fully about these things and perhaps give him the guidance in his attitude towards them which so many today seek and seek in vain. The reading of the story proved a great help to him and we found that it cleared up a number of things which had been puzzling him.

The Lady Anne evidently knew that Willy had been allowed to read the story and hence her allusion to him – when she came in the evening.

August 8th. Early morning.

94

Lady Anne. 'Anne is here (?) Yes, sister, I am here. I stood behind my champion yestereve in your little home
and watched his fair, young son. My heart goes out
to this son of my champion, for I am minded to
picture that my own son might have been such a
one, had he grown to manhood in the body of the
flesh. I have his dear companionship and sonship
now and I am deeply blessed for Elizabeth comes
to me with a daughter's affection at last. Elizabeth
loved me not while she was on earth, and here in
God's open home of love and light, we met not
till of late.'

Then Miss Kelly told me that she had had a message from
Mr Bligh Bond saying that the Lady Anne wished me to hear
her speaking directly to me and that he could arrange a meeting
for me with a direct voice sensitive, Mrs Blanche Cooper at the
Psychic College, London, if I was willing to go.

I was greatly puzzled, I was asked to go to someone I did
not know and to take part in something of which I had never
even heard and was stating my doubt and perplexity to Miss
Kelly when suddenly her hand wrote, 'Expect Anne, but do not
be disappointed if she does not manifest. I who speak am her
brother George. I am commissioned to give any answer if so I
may be enabled to rest your mind on this subject of Anne's wish
to use a medium other than those few friends you are accustomed
to, wilt ask of thy difficulties?'

P.W. 'I have been led during this whole experience step by step
after prayer for guidance and I do not want to do anything
that I am not satisfied I am intended to do.'
G.B. 'Well friend, hast thou ever found that thou hast been led
astray by us on this side of the veil?'
P.W. 'No, but I am also a little anxious about going to a public
meeting, and that harm to myself may come out of it.'
G.B. 'Have no care for self in His service. This meeting we desire is not a public one and thou hast not need to make
known anything about it till such time as God reveals to
thee His own plan. I say again what has been so repeatedly
said to thee and others, have no fear, have no fear; perfect

love must cast out fear. There is a purpose and a place in all that has transpired: do not thou our earthly friend and companion mar the plan, but be content to follow direction when thou hast asked to be directed from on high. I go and give thee my blessing and my grateful thanks for what thou hast done for my dear sister.'

Certainly my thoughts and anxieties had been seen, but could I have imagined that her brother George would have been the one to come and reply to them, and strange to say the words: 'Perfect love casteth out fear', had been very much in my mind, and I had spoken on it in Sulgrave Church just before coming to Hove, but how little I thought it would be given such an application in such a strange way up on the Sussex Downs by the brother of my heroine of four hundred years ago.

The moment George Boleyn stopped speaking I realised that there was something else I had wanted to ask and so I said to Miss Kelly:—

'I meant to ask what was the object of hearing the Lady Anne's voice, when I could not possibly recognise it not having ever heard it before.'

Hardly had I spoken when Miss Kelly gave a kind of sudden involuntary laugh and she shook her head rapidly twice as if to express a negation, and then at once I realised that the Lady Anne was present herself; as Miss Kelly afterwards told me, in her bright happy spirit, so that she could not help laughing with her and catching something of her buoyancy.

Listening to her clairaudiently, Miss Kelly repeated the following words:

'No voice unknown can be recognised, yet I shall make my champion know me, Anne. I come tonight with my brothers, all of them are here and my daughter too, I am pleased to meet your son, will he give me greeting?'

Willy. 'Yes certainly.'

Anne. 'I am indebted to all of you who help us to perform our works of love and ransom.'

E.K. 'She has now gone over beside you and has put her hand on your shoulder and she says:—

Anne. 'My friend, my champion and my charge. Have faith and
confidence and fear nothing. I wish to use the medium
spoken of that my champion may hear my voice and
speak with me face to face. I wish to bring about her a
band of spirits. She can be made a channel by (here the
thread seemed lost) devotional sitters.'

E.K. 'Did you say "devotional sitters"?'

Anne. 'Yes, so few such channels are available. We would enlist
them all for this work only.'

After breakfast we packed up our kit, got on our cycles, said
good-bye to Miss Kelly, and arrived home quite ready for lunch.
Then as soon as possible I related all that had happened to Maud
and she agreed with me that I should go to London, as there
was probably more depending upon it than we knew, and lest,
as George Boleyn had said, I might mar a carefully worked out
plan.

So I sent Miss Kelly a message that I would go with her on
September 2nd and now August 16th I am quietly awaiting
whatever the result may be.

It is a beautiful summer Sunday evening and naturally at the
8 a.m. Holy Communion service in Hove Parish Church, it was
all for me a subject of special thought and prayer and I tried
to make the collect for the day my own desire.

'Let Thy merciful ears O Lord, be open to the prayers of Thy
humble servant, and that he may obtain his petitions, make him
to ask such things as shall please Thee.'

Such things as shall please Thee, that is why I am so cautious
and asking for help and direction at each new step. I have not
sought these experiences, they have as it were been thrust upon
me, I do indeed and in truth only want to do such things as are
pleasing to my Lord.

CHAPTER SEVENTEEN

THE DIRECT VOICE

I kept wondering how the Lady Anne could possibly make her identity known to me, even should she be able to speak directly as she suggested. The only way I could think of was that someone whose voice I could recognise would come first, and then having established her own identity would as it were introduce the Lady Anne or at least guarantee that it was she who spoke.

However as usual, none of my own ideas realised themselves, and something quite unexpected happened which was really more evidential than anything I had thought of.

September 2nd, 1925, was a lovely day and Mrs Crawford Smith a friend of Miss Kelly's who lives at Brighton and is a member of the Brighton Psychic Research Committee, having become interested in the story and being anxious to attend the meeting herself, very kindly offered to drive us up to London in her lovely big Austin car.

Before starting, Maud and I knelt in prayer that all that was done might be in accordance with God's will and purpose.

We reached the Psychic College, Holland Park, at 2.30 p.m. and there we met waiting for us Miss Kelly's great friend Mrs Marriott, who had read my story and had specially come to be present. Mr Bligh Bond also soon came, so we were really a party of friends, six in all.

Then Mrs Mackenzie our hostess came into the waiting room. Mr Mackenzie gave the house for the college and they live there and make it a meeting place for friends as well as a centre for psychic research. As I wished to remain unknown to anyone in the college, I was not introduced to her by name, and I was not wearing clerical dress, but just my ordinary holiday kit.

At 3 p.m. we were shown into a room upstairs where we

met Mrs Blanche Cooper, who shook hands with us all very pleasantly and seemed a very natural person, rather slight and with dark eyes. She asked us to sit down in a half circle and then a musical box was started playing. I sat between Miss Kelly and Mrs Marriott, the latter being next the musical box, and so I was the last but one from Mrs Blanche Cooper, who was at the other end of the half circle; this I fancy was not a good position for me and it was also unfortunate that Mrs Marriott was wearing a wrist watch with an illuminated dial for when the light was turned down, this watch kept showing at times and Miss Kelly afterwards told me that it probably accounted for the fact that practically no psychic lights were seen at our end of the half circle.

Miss Kelly had explained to me beforehand that as in photography light will spoil a negative, so in direct voice mediumship light seems to interfere with or disintegrate the power or vibrations.

When the light was turned down, we were all asked to join hands and to stay quiet or to pray but not to make any sound.

In about a minute there was a voice welcoming us in a strong happy tone and Mrs Cooper said it was her special guide or control called Narda, and this Narda spoke a good deal all through in rather broken English explaining things.

Of course I was only one of six, and when the other voices began to come they began at the other end of the circle nearest the medium and furthest from me. I could however hear almost all that was said, as only one voice spoke at a time, but of course each one in the circle only knew the voice that came to them.

Several lights were seen but not by me and Narda said the light is sent for the clergy. There is a clergy present. Medium does not know, but Narda knows, Narda can see and knows what Medium does not know. This seemed to please her immensely and was rather remarkable as of course Mrs Cooper did not know that a clergyman was present. This light moved about apparently and everyone at last saw it except myself, the one for whom it was sent. I thought it must be because I was so dense psychically, but Miss Kelly told me afterwards that she thought the light from the watch had upset the conditions at our end.

Then Mrs Cooper said: 'The power seems going is there anyone else who wants to meet friends?' So I spoke up and said: 'I have come here at the wish of a certain lady and cannot she come and speak to me as she arranged?'

Then a voice close to me and in front of me said.

'I am standing opposite you now, face to face.' It will be remembered that this expression 'face to face' was used by the Lady Anne when she was trying to plan the meeting. She had then said: 'I wish my champion to hear my voice and speak with me face to face.' (Chapter 3.)

I said: 'But how can I know who you are?' The reply was: 'It is I who have arranged this meeting. Have you not come here by arrangement?'

I then said: 'Yes, but I do not know even now who it is. Can you not tell me who is speaking to me?'

Then there came quite clearly and slowly so that everyone in the circle heard the words:—

'Cham, Cham, Champion. Do you know who I am now?'

I said: 'Yes, I know now who it is.'

That was all she said or had time to say, but immediately Narda said, 'The name Champion is given you as a test, do you know what it means?' And of course I could but reply: 'Yes, I understand it quite well.'

Immediately a much louder voice said: 'The power has gone.' And then Mrs Blanche Cooper turned up the light.

CHAPTER EIGHTEEN

CONFIRMATION

A few days later on September 5th Willy and I visited Miss Kelly at Peacehaven. After tea she lighted a fire as it was quite chilly and she asked us would we mind if a message came not by writing but through her voice as it sometimes did and was quicker and more evidential, and in a few minutes to my own complete surprise, Mr Bennett, Willy's former Master at Trent, was speaking to us himself. Of course I had not known him and therefore could not recognise his voice, but to Willy it was unmistakable and while Miss Kelly retained her own consciousness and knew all that was being said, Willy said that every action of her head and hands as well as the voice, put the identity of his old schoolmaster and friend beyond all question.

I cannot attempt to relate all that he said, but his warm shake hands and greeting of Willy was as though he was present in the flesh and a long conversation took place between Willy and his old and loved Master too long to record but it began:

Mr Bennett. 'Well Willy, dear old chap, you know me?'
Willy. 'I should rather think I do Sir.'
Bennett. 'Well that's capital old chap. Now ask me anything you want and don't delay too long for the power won't last and I shall have to go.'
Willy. 'How do you mean you will have to go?'
Bennett. 'I mean I can't hold on very long to this organism I am using. I won't go out of the room, but this is my first shot at this kind of work, and I'm only a beginner, so fire ahead if there's anything you want to ask.'
Willy. 'Do you ever go to Trent now, Sir?'

Bennett.   'Ever go to Trent! Am I ever away from Trent.
            Everything is not right at Trent . . . . though there's
            a lot of good in it.'

Here Willy's stock of questions seemed suddenly exhausted and
he turned to me and said: 'Daddy, I can't think of anything, do
ask him something.' So I took the opportunity and said: 'Mr
Bennett do you know anything about my story?'

Bennett.   'I know it all. I know too the Lady whom you call the
            Lady Anne, but we don't have any titles on this side,
            we drop all that. Willy (turning to him), I'm not a
            master here, I'm just a learner in the lowest class.'
P.W.   'Yes, I know there are no titles, but I like to call her the
            the Lady Anne for old time courtesy sake.'
Bennett.   'I quite understand your feeling, and I shall call her
            the Lady Anne with you. Yes, I know her and I know
            your daughter too.'
P.W.   'Do you mean Lilian?'
Bennett.   'No, not Lilian. Helen your daughter over here.'
P.W.   'Do you know about the direct voice meeting the other
            day in London?'
Bennett.   'Of course I do, I was at the circle.'
P.W.   'Was it the Lady Anne who spoke to me?'
Bennett.   'Yes, it was the Lady Anne, she was standing in front
            of you the whole time, but she could not get through to
            speak to you until just at the end. That illuminated
            watch upset things. I find it hard to explain, but it
            made a kind of damp mist which drove her back each
            time she tried to speak, but she did in the end get
            through all she wanted in the word Champion.'
P.W.   'Yes, wasn't it a good word to give?'
Bennett.   'She had thought about it a lot and she felt that the
            name Champion would be best as a test of her identity.'
P.W.   'Well, I think it was just "A.1.". But, Mr Bennett, what
            does it all mean, what is this Tudor story of mine all
            leading up to?'
Bennett.   'That I don't know, I cannot tell you, but it is all part
            of a great purpose and this knowledge which is now
            being given to the earth is the greatest subject there is,

the greatest subject on earth or in heaven. And Sir, you must not hide it, and you must let your children know of it.'

P.W. 'Do you mean even the younger ones?'

Bennett. 'Yes, everyone of them (then turning to Willy). Oh, my boy, I envy you, I wish I was young again and had your opportunities and knowledge, you are favoured indeed.'

Willy. 'But you were a medium yourself, were you not Sir?'

Bennett. 'Yes, I was but I didn't know it.'

Willy. 'Am I mediumistic?'

Bennett. 'Everyone has mediumistic powers latent in them but some are more open to development than others.'

P.W. 'I don't think I have any, at least I don't seem to get on with them at all.'

Bennett. 'You may not seem to get on, but you are very impressionable and you are very susceptible to dream influence'.

P.W. 'I don't know. I do dream a good deal, but they are all hotch potch.'

Bennett. 'No they are not all hotch potch: they are not all hotch potch.'

P.W. 'No, they are not all hotch potch, I was wrong to say that.'

Bennett. 'Well, you are very impressionable and I should say your psychic development will be on your dream side.'

Then Willy got into his stride and began a series of questions on the nature of matter and evil. I must not reproduce them here as they have no connection with my story, but I must really give his definition of matter as 'solidified spirit'. Which Willy simply clapped his hands over and said it was 'hot stuff', and what he had always believed and what Spinosa was trying to say all the time, but that Mr Bennett had condensed it all into two words. 'Hot Stuff I call that Sir. And now Sir, do tell me what evil is, is it something in itself or isn't it just the absence of good?'

Bennett. 'There can be no such thing as created evil. Evil is more the unconsciousness of good. Mankind is in a state of evolution and is only in his childhood when he has reached the full measure . . . .' (He hesitated and turning to me) 'You know the quotation Sir, it is in the Book.'

P.W.   'The fulness of the measure of the stature of Christ.'

Bennett. 'Yes, that is it, when mankind has reached the fulness of the measure of Christ, evil will cease to exist.'

I must not attempt to give more. Willy got down a good deal in his notes but it was a really long, deep, earnest talk between the old beloved master with his fuller and deepened knowledge and the young ardent student full of his philosophical problems and enquiries.

It went on I am sure for twenty minutes, and then the master said 'Good-bye,' saying, 'I can't hold on any longer; you see it's a new kind of stunt for me, but it isn't too bad for a first shot.'

Willy.   'Jolly good I call it Sir.'

Bennett. 'Well, I'm glad I was able to reach you old chap. Good-bye.'

N.B. Willy after taking an honours degree in Trinity College, Dublin, entered the Colonial Service in Fiji and was doing brilliantly when he was stung in the neck by a hornet and died within a few days of March 26th, 1932, aged 28.

His body was laid to rest on Easter morning in the British Cemetery at Suva, in a beautiful spot like a beautiful garden by the sea.

CHAPTER NINETEEN

THE LAMENT OF ANNE BOLEYN

As I sit down once again to add apparently yet another part to my story, I am struck by the strange way in which new friends and fresh sensitives seem called in to render their help.

Mrs Clegg played the leading part in the beginning, then Miss Kelly is used, while Mrs Hester Dowden's gifts are also called upon. Later Mrs Blanche Cooper and Mrs Crawford Smith are asked to lend their aid, and now to my great surprise an entirely new personality – Mrs Monson comes to our aid.

There has been no possibility of collusion between them for they were either unknown, or practically unknown to one another as well as unknown beforehand to me. Miss Kelly, who took up the story from Mrs Clegg, had never met her, nor had she met Mrs Hester Dowden, while Mrs Blanche Cooper had not met the others: indeed I think they were all quite unknown to each other.

They were quite unconscious that they were actors in a prolonged drama and only afterwards learned of the part they have played, and yet they never seem to make a mistake or to introduce the different characters at a wrong stage in the development of the story.

Besides this, they had no special interest in the Tudor period, they knew nothing of my own interest in it and yet, at the very outset Mrs Clegg can tell the names of the brothers of the Lady Anne which I did not know myself: can accurately describe her coronation procession, even to the colour of the palfrey led behind her chair and knows that there is a close connection between Anne and the Duke of Buckingham and that she had had a misunderstanding with her sister.

A sceptical friend has suggested that she could have found all that information in books. Could she? It took me months to verify it and besides she was not sitting for a special examination of the Tudor period and had no idea beforehand that she was going to be called upon to answer these difficult questions or give information on these intricate and long forgotten points.

Nothing has ever strengthened my faith in Our Lord's resurrection so much as reading the various theories by which it is thought to explain it away, and the more I hear of attempts to explain this story on the supposition that it is not real, the more I lean to the conclusion that the Tudor people who enter into it are realities.

The difficulties of any other explanation are still further increased by the entrance of this new actor into Part IV.

Mrs Monson, whom I have not yet met, is a lady who lives at Brighton and who is possessed of psychic gifts only just developing, and it seemed to me so incredible that she could have written *The Lament of Anne Boleyn* (see Chap. 1) without some special knowledge of her history or without any previous conversation with Miss Kelly or someone else about my story, that I wrote to Miss Kelly on receiving *The Lament* and had the following reply:

> I first met Mrs Monson on January 30th of this year (1925). I do not remember ever mentioning *anything* about your story and Theo (Mrs Monson), is sure I did not, and when she got *The Lament* she knew nothing at all, she is sure, of my interest in the Lady Anne or of any connection with that period or you. The day she first told me about *The Lament* she hesitated to do so in case I should not be interested or think it was all imagination. She desires to use her gifts for good only and she has developed a power of clairvoyance and clairaudience much more since we have known each other. She used to be a little frightened of it, and now she is not, but glad to be able to see or hear.

I wrote also to Mrs Monson herself asking if she would kindly tell me how she first came into contact with the Lady Anne, and whether she knew anything beforehand which would account for the *Lament,* and I have just had from her a long and most interesting reply from which I shall now make some extracts.

December 8th, 1925.

Dear Mr Pakenham-Walsh,

I just want to tell you about my coming to know Miss Kelly and also getting into touch with the Lady Anne.

Last January my husband had an operation in London, and after that Miss Kelly came to give him some magnetic healing treatment; a friend of mine suggested her coming. I had been rather anxious, to tell the truth, about her coming, knowing that she was a medium – there are mediums and mediums – but she told me she was also a nurse, and I soon saw how wise she was and how absolutely one could trust her and all my fears went.

Mrs Monson then goes on to tell how as a girl she could read character through psychometry and handwriting and also that she seemed to possess a certain power of foresight. She then continues:

. . . . But I shrank from developing any powers given me and I had not even when I met Miss Kelly made up my mind whether communion with the unseen was right or wrong, and the whole subject alarmed me. I felt I would be terrified if I saw any phenomena or anyone from the other side. One curious thing had happened, *i.e.* I had suddenly written little poems during the last two years, which as a rule I never could do. This power would come perhaps for a few weeks and then go *absolutely*. I gradually came, as I saw more of E.K. (Eleanor Kelly), to love the thought of the next world and to lose my fears, and one day my mother and elder brother came to me through her and gave me a very beautiful message. I have never been to a seance and I can't honestly say I want to. I can't bear the table rapping, planchette, etc., etc. – but E.K. has explained in her wonderfully clear common-sense way that we have sometimes to make use of material means.

Well, it wasn't till about last April that I began to feel that the poetry was being put into my mind by some outside influence and then I seemed to see, not with the physical eyes but with the eye of the mind, people, and to receive first poetry through them and then one or two messages.

E.K. did tell me that she was doing some special work, and I vaguely heard of her having to go up to London but she never mentioned your name to me and she never mentioned that this work had anything to do with the Tudors, in fact I hadn't the slightest idea what the work was about.

Then *The Lament of Anne Boleyn* suddenly came to me one day in September. It was not automatic writing, I haven't ever done this, nor did I at first sense any presence. It came into my mind and I wrote it down just as it came, sometimes hesitating for a word, which came after a little waiting.

While writing, I did seem to see the figure of a woman in

the dress of that period, velvet and silk and a little head-dress of velvet and pearls coming to a point on the forehead, a very sweet gracious smile and sunny brown hair.

E.K. came to see me one day soon after and I felt rather dubious really as to even showing her *The Lament* I thought it so very bad really, and not fit to show to anyone and yet I could not understand why it should come into my head.

When I mentioned the name Anne Boleyn to her, I was really startled, because she was so amazed and kept saying: 'Are you sure we never talked to you or mentioned her name' and I could most faithfully say: 'Never'.

Here there is a clear statement from both these ladies that they had not communicated at all about the Lady Anne or my story before the Lady Anne appeared to Mrs Monson and before the *Lament* was written.

Also one has Mrs Monson's declaration that she is not at all well versed in the Tudor period, and yet she commences at once to write the most dramatic scenes introducing Tudor personages with a vividness and reality which would make her name as a tragedian.

Her explanation is that she sees the personages of whom she speaks, hears what they say either to her or to one another and writes it down, and if this is not the true explanation, then what other can be suggested?

She could have no purpose in carrying on a deliberate fraud: she gains nothing from it, and her letter is so simple and straightforward as to disarm suspicion. She has not the historical knowledge nor the dramatic ability to write of such scenes. She is not what is popularly known as a spiritualist or medium, she has never been to a seance. Her whole time is devoted to an invalid husband and life for her is too strenuous and serious to spend in unrealities. Now can telepathy explain it; the Lady Anne appears to her and impresses her to write the *Lament* before she knows anything of me or has any interest in the subject.

It is just on a par with so much more in this strange experience, inexplicable unless we accept the seemingly normal and yet supernormal solution.

And now having said my say and introduced my new friend Mrs Monson – or T.M. as she calls herself for short – let us read *The Lament*.

Ah! Woe is me – pent up within this sullen Tower,
Bereft of love, of hope, and soon bereft of life itself;
Though that were scarcely hardship – to escape from this!
This death in life, this hourly drawn out agony of terror
Still to come. Yet 'tis not many hours since I did hear
The rusty bars withdrawn, and saw the heavy door
Of my imprisonment flung wide, but not, alas, for me!
But to admit the entry of some dour faced men,
Governor, Janitor, of courtiers of His Majesty's.
Within they filed, so many men, so many swords,
So many frowning looks, to face one poor weak woman
        child,
And once their Queen.
Forsooth I hardly listened while they spake
And unrolled heavy parchment,
And with harsh discordant voice, one read aloud
My sentence – I suppose of death!
My thoughts were far away, and I was strolling once again
About the pleasaunces of Hampton Court,
Or listening to the flatteries, the smooth-tongued whispers
        of those very men – some of them!
I recollect now one had need of favour
To procure some influential post, and therefore to his
        Queen
Then nearest to his Sovereign's pliable heart, he hied him
On bended knee, with honeyed phrase he pleaded
To me, his Queen, that I should intercede,
Should gain my husband's ear for him. My husband!
Great God, Whom I neglected in my days of fame,
Oh, hear me now I beg Thee – I beseech
Did ever wretched girl repent as I have
Through these haunted days and nights?
Repent! Why, I have grovelled on the stony floor
And torn my hair, those tresses once by Royal hands
        caressed,
Whose head lay on his breast – I shudder at the thought.
But listen, God, dear God, for in truth it seemeth
In my dire plight, Thou are indeed my only Friend,
If mercy Thou wilt have! I meant no harm,
I was a giddy child, fair to men's eyes,
Loving the glitter, the magic of a Throne.
My head was turned by foolish flattery,
Those round me whispered, hinted, urging me to folly,
Talk of Royal favour, for their own ends, methinks!
Since I have lain these weary days alone
My sight has clearer grown, and I have seen into men's
        thoughts,

The mists of vanity and pride have faded
The veil of glamour rent in twain!
Stript bare of jewels, silks, my Royal lover, friends so-
    called,
Dragged through the mire of calumny dishonoured,
    disgraced
My poor body, once by men called fair.
Now ravished, scorned, nigh trodden underfoot,
And yet my soul they cannot touch
'Tis all that's left me, empty though it be.
At length these gloomy, dour faced men, hearing my
    sentence read
Demanded if I aught desired? had aught to say?
Some plea of sorrow for my sins, some abject message to
    my King?
I raised my head and with an effort brought my scattered
    thoughts
Back from these gardens fair, the Rout, the Ball and by-
    gone memories,
And gazed for the last time on those faces, once so
    wreathed in smiles,
Lips that had touched their Majesty's fair hand in homage,
Tongues that had lied, ah me! And then the blood
Rushed to my head, and once again a Queen I stood
Erect with flashing eye and heaving bosom,
With outstretched hand I cried—words that seemed given
Me to speak—that must be spoken:—

    Farewell, my lords, Farewell!
    Thy Queen has need of no interpreter
    She goes where secrets are laid bare, to where her
        King
    The King of all the World her judge will be.
    'Vengeance is mine,' Thus saith my God
    Now is thine audience ended. Thou mayst go.

Like craven hounds with tails between their legs
And eyes averted, they slunk out one by one,
And the door clanged behind them.
For a brief space I stayed uplifted, head held high
Then, thought of where I was returned,
My spirit shrank, my heart gave way.
I flung myself upon the stony floor again in agony of tears.
Why had I said those words? Did I believe them?
What were they to me? I wanted life,
All that a woman cares for—happiness, love!
I, so young, so beautiful, men and my mirror said;
Yet must I die? And what comes after death?

And so I've lain, heedless of chill and deepening dusk
Alone, but for my thoughts.
I am so tired, so weary, had I but some friend,
A hand to hold, someone to smooth the way!
I must not think of what's to come,
I dare not, of the morrow, lest I go mad with sudden
    horror.
Oh! My heart beats now so fast, the terror chokes me,
My God, dear God, I do intreat Thee, save me.
I am so weak. Think of the morrow, the crowds,
Their grinning faces; me, their Queen, led forth to die.
The awful block, the axe, No, No!
I dare not be alone through this dread night.
Will no one come? I'm fainting, ill,
My teeth are chattering, Oh! Will no one come!
A knock? Surely I heard it. Oh! Come in, come in.
Whoe'er it be. I'd welcome e'en my bitterest foe
Tonight, rather than be alone. Come in.
Oh! Father, holy Father, is it Thou? Oh, I am glad,
    am glad
Thank God for sending thee – nay, I must kneel, I am
    distraught
Fear not these tears, they bring relief! And thou wilt
    stay
All night. Thou wilt not leave me! O father
How I bless thee; See, I am no more a Queen,
But just a helpless child. Sit here! Yes – I entreat,
Upon my wretched bed, and I will kneel to thee
And my Confession make. The story of a foolish reckless
    girl,
Who bartered all for power, for wealth – a throne!
Played with men's hearts, perchance,
But lightly, father, not with ill intent.
Oh! how I shiver! 'Tis with lying on that floor,
Thou offerest me thy cloak! Honour for me
Not thee, kind father. Yea indeed
I'll gladly wrap it round and warm myself!
There! Now wilt thou listen to this erring child,
Holding my mind, my cold cold hand
And teach me how to die.

Now let me lean my head upon thy knee
My father kind, and close mine eyes
I am so weary, yet I fain would strive
My foolish errors to recall. Alas! I cannot think
No words will come save only : 'God forgive me',
Save one despairing cry : 'God help me

Through this dreadful end, and shorten pain
And give me courage, for I am – or was – a Queen
And as a Queen would meet the end, howe'er unjust
With dignity – and faith and hope – Ah me'.
What says't thou father? That it is enough?
I need not tell thee more? Nor rack my weary head
My aching brain for all my many faults.
That through the Saviour, crucified upon the Cross
My sins are all forgiven, as I must forgive
Those who have slandered me. Forgive those traitors!
Who betrayed me to the King! Forgive the King!
Who turned upon the thing he'd loved, had made his
    Queen,
And himself planned my downfall!

The Saviour died, thou sayest. He forgave those
Who betrayed Him. He died with thieves
Thieves on each side of Him. He who had no sin
The meanest death of most prolonged agony!
Whilst I! O father! He who had no fault; forgave,
Then how much more must I who am so full
Of faults, forgive!
O blessed Peace that fills my soul
Support me to the end, uphold me with Thy grace.
Yet not the end, as thou has taught me, father,
But rather the beginning of the life with Him.
If I have lost all else beside, friends, wealth, position,
Earthly love; my emptied soul is filled with Thee
My Saviour and Thy love Divine.
Mine eyes are opened and methinks I see
The things of earth pass like some puppet show;
I view them from afar. A little patience, and the show
    is o'er,
The curtain falls, and thou, kind father, will be near.
To hold the Cross and point me to the skies?
So that I shall not heed the dreadful block,
The grinning crowd, nor see the axe,
Save as the Key that openeth wide the door
Into my Saviour's home, where I shall dwell
The lowest of His children – but with Him.

Perchance in days to come these words of mine
May flow through human agent back to earth
Whereon I suffered so? May take some message –
Ring some echo still for Anne Boleyn.
Nay father, deem me not self-seeking, chide me not.
But I would have men know the once 'light' Queen

Was not all heartless – that at least her death
In trust with God, was not unqueenlike, if her living was.
Now let me sleep – I am so tired – against thy knee,
Thy hand upon my head in blessing laid,
I am so young. He was my King . . . . my husband,
So I thought , . . . Was it a dream?
Could I but wake in Heaven . . . . a little child . . . .
    once more.

Note: I had always thought that the Lament was based on an
imaginary visit of some 'Courtiers' to the Queen in her prison
and it was not till 1956, some 30 years later, that to my surprise and astonishment I found a full account of it in the
Lives of Two Queens by Hepworth Dixon (*Vol. IV p.* 318).
    Norfolk, her judge, with some of those who had con-
demned her to death did actually visit them both in prison,
seeking first to get a confession of guilt from George Boleyn
and failing with him went on to the cell of the Queen telling
her that she would do better to confess her fault. 'They
talked of what the King had done for her,' but the Queen
replied, 'All that is past, I have done nothing against the
King. And I have laid down everything the King has given
me. I am now no more than Anne Boleyn. My lords on my
salvation I have committed no offence.'

    No wonder—
        'Like craven hounds with tails between their legs,
        And eyes averted, they slunk out one by one,
        And the door clanged behind them.'

CHAPTER TWENTY

THE LADY ANNE BOLEYN

After Mrs Monson had been impressed to write the *Lament* and had shown it to Miss Kelly, the latter then for the first time spoke of me to her and also lent her my Play and Story to read.

They came to her not only, as was now natural, as a great interest, but the story proved to her a real spiritual help, specially as she was passing through a very difficult time, owing to a serious operation which her husband had undergone. While her heart was filled with this new wonder and joy, suddenly the Lady Anne stands beside her and the scene which follows is to my mind so tender and beautiful that short though it be, I am placing it in this chapter by itself and giving it exactly in Mrs Monson's own words, and prefaced and concluded by short explanatory notes.

> I would like to copy out this, which I received on Thursday last, November 19th, 1925, after praying for help and guidance very earnestly, that I might be shown my duty in the matter of receiving messages from those on the other side.
>
> T. H. E. Monson. (T.M.)

Lady Anne. 'It is I, friend, dear child – Anne. I am so glad it has helped you – the reading of my faithful champion's words.'

T.M. 'I do so want to believe it is really you, Lady Anne.'

Lady Anne. 'And now I *am* here, thou canst not believe, doubting one, even after the Lord's blessing.'

T.M. 'I so fear it lies within my heart's imagination which does so long to see and talk with you.'

Lady Anne. 'No, no, it is true. Now write. Thou are connected with me in some way I cannot now explain, but the way will be made clear. Accept any texts and messages, always with prayer, for thou hast much to cloud and oppress thy mind and judgment at present. This we know and would fain help thee to overcome and withstand. It is thy Cross. Nay, weep not dear one, child, child, thou must be brave. Thou shalt be released soon : only be calm and have patience. Hast thou not felt our presence and our pity? Nay, not pity –Love ! The power grows dim. Do not sorrow. I go now; with another I will return anon. Conditions are not good now.'

This visit of the Lady Anne does not seem to me to be at all the kind of scene which Mrs Monson would have made up herself. She admits that she is desirous to see the Lady Anne, which she would not say if she was writing for copy, and the whole interview rings true.

For the Lady Anne to come just after the help and emotion set up by reading her story is most natural and of course the sympathy aroused would psychologically open the pathway.

It is a very tender scene this sister from the land of light and peace bringing comfort and courage to the earth sister in her trouble.

The letter was sent on to me by Miss Kelly and I then wrote myself to Mrs Monson telling her how pleased I was that my story had proved of such help to her and how interested I was to know that she was being called in to co-operate. I then asked her to describe the Lady Anne as she saw her and I had the following reply:—

. . . . You ask me to describe Lady Anne. It is a very sweet, gracious presence, which brings the feeling of happiness and charm and love. I have seen her in a dress somewhat similar to the Holbein Queen Katherine which I enclose, but the headdress is not so heavy and I always see soft curls of bright brown hair and shining dark brown eyes and a rose complexion and shining mouth. Then again I have seen her in white satin or silk; her dark hair (no–not dark, brown with gleams of gold in it), only covered with red and white roses and carrying roses –a beautiful picture ! I can't recollect ever having seen a portrait of her in my life.

This description tallies with her pictures and with practically all the accounts we have of her, but Mrs Monson had not seen a picture of her.

The clairvoyants are not in a league of deceit; they do not

know each other and have never met. They had not specially
studied up the Tudor period, in fact they both frankly confess
they know but little about it and yet they both declare that they
see a figure quite plainly who speaks to them and they both
describe the Lady Anne Boleyn in all particulars correctly according both to her pictures and the accounts we have of her.

With the entrance of yet another sensitive into the Tudor
Arena, those who have read so far will have realised that there
is running through this strange story a deep purpose, not just the
vindication of an innocent woman, but the bringing home to
those who caused her death, not only a realisation of their own
wrong doing but also a creation in their hearts of a desire to seek
of mercy and forgiveness from the God whom they had either
forgotten or denied.

This apparently could only be accomplished by the co-operation of those on both sides of the Veil as has already been seen
in Chap. VII and now again is brought through the psychic gifts
of Theodore Monson and Eleanor Kelly in a series of vision or
experience in which the actors see themselves as they really are.
It would make this chapter too long to record them all, and so
only four are here described under the title of:—

HENRY AND KATHERINE.

CHAPTER TWENTY-ONE

HENRY AND KATHERINE

The very next day as Mrs Monson was alone and in bed she suddenly became aware of King Henry's figure near her and Henry at once spoke.

Henry R. 'It is I. I am here. Henry Rex' (very loudly), 'write as thou didst before. What controls this power thou hast? How comes it I can speak to thee without open voice and that thou canst hear?'

T.M. 'I only know it is so Henry, and you will soon know far more than I.'

Henry R. 'Dost thou always remain here?'

T.M. 'Oh, no. What can I do for you?'

Henry R. 'There is one thing I would ask, one matter requiring my royal attention' (said with hands on hips and very haughtily), 'Nay, I am forgetful. I am no longer a king. I cannot find the right words' (he seemed so distressed and perplexed), 'and words, odd words will come.'

He was quiet a moment and then tried again quite humbly.

'There is a matter, but I cannot find the words.' (He put his hand to his head sighing.)

T.M. 'Couldst thou not ask and of others nearer, Queen Katherine perhaps?'

Henry R. 'No, no it is not seemly or fit. Could I speak to *him* that—' (interruption came here for a few minutes but almost as soon as I was alone, Henry was there again). 'I would continue. I would speak to the holy father, the priest. Could I speak to him?'

T.M.   'Yes, at least I will ask him to arrange it, but it may take time.'

Henry R.   'What is time? I do not wish to wait. But there, it is all different now. I am not to be considered, my wishes do not count, as when I could sever heads at a glance almost.' (He saw my look of sorrow and dismay.) 'Thou likest not such talk? I will not again. I did not mean to say that. I will go now but how shall I know?'

T.M.   'Canst thou not pray? Find comfort in prayer, Henry. That will guide thee.'

Henry R.   'I will pray. Tell the holy father I have found some relief, but if he truly serves my God, as Defender of the Faith I would speak again with him, as soon as . . . . as . . . . he can. I . . . , I . . . . would not disturb him' (spoken slowly and with difficulty and some emotion) 'but I . . . . *need* him. Now I go, I thank thee. Thou hast been courteous to one who suffers – I go.'

A fortnight later, December 1st, at about 5 p.m. Mrs Monson was conscious of a figure near her and she said: 'I think it is Queen Katherine?'

Katherine.   'Yes, it is, for Henry, my poor Henry I come, but not as Queen, friend – as sister.'

T.M.   'What may I do?'

Katherine.   'Wilt thou take a message from Henry.' (Interruption.) 'I am here again, but not very clear is the line. Wait. Now that is better. Anne's champion, will he remember at the Early Celebration, my poor Henry. An opportunity later will be given –' (interruption again).

T.M.   'I am so sorry.'

Katherine.   'We will try again. An opportunity will be afforded the holy father to speak closely to Henry.' (Interruption – called away to attend my sick husband.)

T.M.   'Forgive the discourtesy, dear Lady. He little knew that I was entertaining Royalty!'

Katherine.   'I had best say quickly what I have to say. This is not a good time but the channel is open and thou receptive.

T.M. 'Yes, I felt so.'

Katherine. 'Tell the holy father, Henry is less vindictive, less morose. He even shows some interest on this side and realises clearly at times where he is. We need his co-operation, yes, Henry's, in what has to be revealed and cannot accomplish our work until the clouds are lifted from his soul:—the weight of pride, greed, cruelty; oh! I would not speak much of all that, it brings back what is best forgotten. Yet, for our purpose this must at times be recalled. Farewell, I must go.'

HENRY'S ANGER

I include this episode in my Tudor Story because I believe that it shows very clearly how closely our plans and interests in this world are known to those in the next.

I had been chosen as one of the delegates from the diocese of Peterborough to go to a conference at Westminster in January 1926. At this time Shakespeare's play *Henry VIII* was being performed, and Mrs Monson had promised to procure some complimentary tickets for the evening performance. I wrote to Miss Kelly suggesting we meet at Mrs Marriott's house at 3 p.m., as there was so much I wanted to ask about the progress being made by Henry VIII and the other Tudor personages.

Owing to various complications it was impossible for me to carry out this plan, and at the last minute I had to accept tickets to the afternoon performance, thus postponing our meeting with Henry until the evening.

We reached Mrs Marriott's flat about 6 p.m., and were joined there by a clergyman and his wife who were interested in my story, and were most sympathetic.

The first person to speak was Sir Thomas Boleyn, who came to thank me for all that I had done for his daughter, and to confess his own part in her tragedy, caused by his worldly ambitions.

As soon as he had finished speaking Henry VIII came and demanded in tones of terrible anger why I had broken my appointment with him.

I explained that I had not meant to break my appointment, but that I had not realised that by changing my plan I had unwittingly upset the arrangements evidently made by the Lady Anne to bring the Tudor personages to us in the afternoon.

Henry R. 'Don't tell me that. You broke it so that you might go to the theatre to mock. You have been scoffing and mocking me all the afternoon!'

P.W. 'I was not scoffing at you, Henry, I was sympathising with you.'

Henry R. 'Don't talk to me like that. I will not put up with it. You were scoffing at me. I tell you that I will not stand it. I will not brook such insult and disobedience. I will not put up with it in you or any other. . . .'

Here the torrent of wrath and abuse suddenly stopped to my amazement and relief, and putting his hands to his head in a bewildered way, he said slowly and quietly:—

'I did not come here to say this. Oh! what am I saying? Oh, what have I said! I am a poor, miserable confounded sinner, a poor wretched damned soul, a sinner sunk in hell.'

He paused, and I asked what I could do to help him.

Henry R. 'I want advice. I am surrounded with all those wenches howling and wailing after me. Why should they be howling after me now? What am I to do for them?'

I suggested that the only path for him was to take these people one by one and find out what the trouble was, and try to put it right.

Henry R. 'Face each one by one! How can I? There would be no end of them and I cannot face them all.'

After admitting that Queen Katherine, the Lady Anne, and Lord Rochford had all forgiven him he went on:—

Henry R. '. . . . there is one wench always wailing after me.'
(Jane Seymour.) 'She has injured me. She sinned
against me. She committed a great crime against –'
(with great anger) 'she kept back papers from me. I
can never forgive her, never, never. I detest her.'

Rev. X. 'If you forgive not men their trespasses, neither will
your Heavenly Father forgive you yours.'

P.W. 'Henry, remember the words of the Lord Jesus on
the Cross, "Father forgive them for they know not
what they do".'

Henry R. (Furious.) 'Don't talk to me like that. You won't
deceive me. She did know what she did. She did
know it.'

I explained that she was sorry and wanted to confess, but
that he would not give her an opportunity.

Henry R. (Rising with passion and standing over me in a most
threatening attitude.) 'I tell you, I will not receive her
confession. I loathe and detest and abominate the
woman, and I shall not permit her to approach me.'

I asked if he could not be more gentle to her, remembering that
she was the mother of his son Edward.

Henry R. (Collapsing on the seat and putting his hands over
his eyes.) 'Where is my son? Oh, where is my son?
Why is my son kept from me? Give me back my son
and I will forgive her.'

P.W. 'Henry, do you really want your son back to you in
all your darkness and misery? You would not really
wish it. No, Henry, he cannot come back to you, but
you may go to him if only you will be gentle and
penitent.'

When Mrs Marriott made a remark while Henry was still
speaking he asked petulantly—

Henry R. 'Who is that? What are all these people doing? Why
do you bring all these witnesses about me?'

I tried to explain that we all wanted to help him, I begged

him to take the help and advice we offered, not to let the opportunity slip by.

Henry R. 'You have helped me and I am grateful. Yes, I will forgive. Here, Katherine' (turning and putting out his hand), 'lead me to Jane.'

It was a great encounter and what doubtless turned it in my favour was my appeal to him to be gentle to Jane as the mother of his son Edward. It was the strongest appeal I could have made to him.

I cannot imagine why Henry should be so bitter against Jane Seymour. Historians all say that she was the wife whom he liked best, or rather, perhaps, with whom he did not fall out; and his body was laid beside hers in St George's Chapel, Windsor – I believe at his own request.

CHAPTER TWENTY-TWO

HENRY AND WOLSEY

Between February 19th and February 26th, there were one or two warnings that Henry wanted to come to me again but nothing came of them.

T.M.

Henry R. 'Woman, woman.'

T.M. 'Is it Henry?'

Henry R. 'It is Henry and thou hast denied me speech some days. Why didst thou not answer before?'

T.M. 'I am very sorry Henry. You must forgive me. I have been very tired.'

Henry R. 'Tired? What is tired? I know not, except of this, this uncertainty.'

T.M. 'Comest thou in the name of God?'

Henry R. 'Yes, I do come in the name of God, but why askest thou that question?'

T.M. 'I wanted to make sure.'

Henry R. 'Doubting again? There is no doubt, alas, though at times so bewildered am I, I might well doubt myself! Woman' (coming close to my bedside), 'where is Eleanor? Hath she not been here? Callest thou not her by that name, Eleanor?'

T.M. 'Yes, that is her name: she has been here today but is, I think, safe in her own bed now.'

Henry R. 'Thou dost not know where my sons are? I did see them, but for a brief space. Eleanor and a right likely fellow brought me, but I may not be with them always yet, dost thou think Eleanor would pray that I might be with my sons? Woman, woman I cannot reward thee as once I could but things are different here.' (Then I sensed a very sad but dignified

123

presence and saw Cardinal Wolsey, Henry also saw him.) 'Woman, dost thou know who this is, who has honoured thee' (very sarcastically) 'by coming to see thee?'

T.M.   'I think it is Cardinal Wolsey.'

Wolsey.   'I am that sad and sorrowful one and yet not wholly sad, for my Master hath given me work to do for him. He hath shown tender mercy to His erring child.'

Henry R.   'Why comest thou when *I* am here? It is an intrusion; thou shouldest ask permission before thou intrudest thus.'

Wolsey.   'Henry, thou owest me this. I did great wrong for thee on earth for which I now do penance. Had I refused to pander to thy vices, thy wishes perchance I had not sunk to the low depths I did.'

G. Boleyn.   'Theo, I am here. I brought Wolsey. Can you speak to Henry?'

Henry R.   (Sulkily.) 'Thou shouldest not have brought him, George Boleyn, thou takest too much upon thyself! I, I do not feel I can look upon him yet' (half turns back on Wolsey), 'it brings too much to remembrance.' (Slowly and very low, as if to himself.) ''Tis too much, I cannot bear the weight,' (moving away). 'Woman, why dost thou not send this priest away? I like not his presence' (pitifully), 'must I bear with him too?'

T.M.   'Henry, love has been born in thy heart for thy wives, thy sons; canst thou not forgive another? Thou owest him much. If he forgives thee, be not less forgiving.'

Henry R.   'Nay, how shouldst thou know what need there is for me to forgive? Thou wast not of my time. I comprehend it not,' (shaking head and looking very puzzled). 'Oh, woman, if thou hast a woman's heart like Katherine – like Anne . . . . Why there is Anne!' (And I was at once conscious of her between Henry and Wolsey in radiant white.)

Anne.   'Greeting to my friend Theo.'

T.M.   'Comest thou in the name of God?'

Anne.   (Bending head.) 'I do so come Theo and on His work am I here tonight. Thou dost right to try me, if thou wert doubtful. Henry, have mercy as others have shewn mercy to thee and forgiveness.'

Henry R. (Most piteously still with back turned to her and Wolsey.) 'Anne, I cannot, I cannot – spare me. The sight of him brings back so much torment. I suffer so, I – I –' (falls upon his knees).

Wolsey.   (Putting out his hands as if in blessing.) 'Did ever these hands of mine yearn more greatly to bless, but unworthy am I, 'tis for my Master to comfort this poor soul in like plight as I.'

G. Boleyn. 'Theo, help them. I have brought them not easily.'

T.M.   'Our Lord help me to say what is right. May He look down upon these two souls and comfort them.' (Here I saw a beautiful angel near Henry, stooping over him with long golden hair and wings.)

Angel.   'Henry, Henry, the Master calleth thee. Come with me and I will lead thee to Him! But first bid farewell to thy friends for a while.'

Henry R. 'Shall I not return? I cannot go to him,' (covering his face with his hands), 'I, I denied Him. I am no great king but a poor worthless man.'

(All this time the Lady Anne, Wolsey and George Boleyn were praying with hands and eyes uplifted.)

Henry R. 'I would go to my Father but I know not the way. Lead me to Him then, but I .... Woman,' (turning to me imploringly). 'What must I do? Tell me, I feel .... my heart .... 'twill break!'

T.M.   'Go with the Heavenly Guide, Henry as she bids thee, fearing nothing, and speak thy heart out to the Lord Jesus thy Saviour, and thou wilt receive comfort.'

Henry R. (Quite humbly), 'I thank thee, I will go.'

The angel took him away, one gentle hand on his shoulder. Wolsey then turned and gave me a sad but peaceful smile and then was gone too. Anne too had gone, but I was still aware of George Boleyn.

G. Boleyn. 'Pray for these two souls Theo, for Henry and Wolsey, that they may be reconciled and become friends. The Master sent the help, Theo, the Lord Jesus Christ, we are only His messengers. God be with thee, Theo, now, and give thee peace.'

Henry had evidently passed on into higher hands and may not again need help in the same way from earth, and on March 5th, 1926, Miss Kelly had this short message from Katherine, after some other messages had been spoken:—

'I too, Katherine, am full happy dear sister, woman, in the cleansing of my love, my heart's king, my Henry, the Father of my children.
Bless thee and all, each one, for the loving help, the uniting with us in our labour of dear love.
Christ be with us.'

CHAPTER TWENTY-THREE

HENRY MEETS HIS SONS

On the same night February 18th, as the last scene was taking place but earlier by a few hours, another act in the drama took place before or through Miss Kelly, which I will now copy from Miss Kelly's letter, dated February 22nd:

I will try now to tell you as well as I can, my experience on the night of Thursday, February 18th.

I know how suggestible mediumship is and how carefully we need to guard ourselves in receiving impressions. This frame of mind was strong upon me and I was feeling anxious in case errors should creep in and confuse the issue, not doubting T.M. one whit more than myself, only praying we might both be clear channels.

Then at 9.45 I was aware of Henry standing by my side, a different and quite gentle Henry, with no arrogance of manner or temper about him. He came close to my shoulder and said in a puzzled tone : 'Woman, why dost thou doubt thy friend?' I said I was not doubting my friend any more than myself and could not explain my thought to him. Then he said : 'It doth confuse me, it doth confuse me; one saith this and another that. *Who* is thy friend? Who *is* this holy father? Who are *thou*?'

I answered : 'Just men and women like you and yours, ordinary human people who only want to be friendly and help one another.'

Then he bent down to look closely at my face and said :

'Thou art that one who first did call me; *thou* it was who led me to my Kate, lead me now to my sons. I was told I might find my sons with thee. Jane – Jane ever talketh of a crime, a crime, what is one crime among so many; I cannot wait to listen of her crime, all was crime !'

Just then I knew Dick was with me, and suddenly Henry saw him and looked at him with astonishment, then said slowly almost with awe : 'He shines, he shines, woman is he thy son?'

'No, but like a son to me. I have no children of my own. I never married.'

Henry R. (Vehemently.) 'Woman, thou *shouldest* marry and
   bear sons.'

Then we talked a little and he asked questions about unborn babies and again kept saying : 'My sons, find me my
sons.'

Then Dick bent down and whispered to me : 'Oh, Auntie,
tell him, Anne's son *is* here, tell him, make him see.'

I told Henry what Dick said and he looked from one to
the other of us and round about and then all at once, he saw
his own son, and such a look came into his eyes I could not
watch him or say a word or make any note, his face changed
completely and when he spoke again he said things I can't
repeat, about his former visits and having once held out his
hand for me to kiss, and then he knelt down beside me and
took my hand and kissed it once, tears were running down his
face but he took no notice of it and stood looking at the son,
not touching him or speaking.

(Readers will remember that this is the son of the Lady Anne
born (still-born), in February 1536 after the shock of her meeting Henry with Jane Seymour.)

Then Anne came too and his other son (Edward, Jane Seymour's son), and poor Jane came and stood near them.

Henry and Jane were wrapt in a dull sort of grey colour like
fog, dark and heavy. Anne and the two sons were perfectly
beautiful, covered with a shining light. Each of the boys took
his own mother by the hand and the two mothers took each one
hand of Henry's, Jane hanging back timidly, and they, the
sons and Anne, led Henry and Jane step by step up a height,
and as they climbed Henry and Jane seemed to grow lighter
and purer, and they passed out of my sight.

And so another step forward has been gained and Henry
has at least seen his sons who appear to be so much to him.

CHAPTER TWENTY-FOUR

LADY ROCHFORD

Students of the Tudor period may remember that it was the false witness of Lady Rochford, wife of George Boleyn, which was mainly responsible for the death both of her husband and also of his sister the Lady Anne. A few years later she became involved with Queen Katherine Howard and was executed with her, confessing her crime on the scaffold (saying that she supposed God had permitted her to suffer this shameful doom as a punishment for her false accusation of Queen Anne Boleyn. (Agnes Strickland.)

In most of these scenes I was simply the recorder of what Theodore Monson or Eleanor Kelly told me they witnessed but on October 4th, 1926, while I was on a visit with Mrs Crawford Smith in Brighton and was alone with Eleanor Kelly when she saw a woman coming apparently in great misery and Miss Kelly felt a sick sensation and pain round her neck and I felt sure it was Lady Rochford and I cannot help thinking that she would not come or speak until we were alone, and no wonder, for she began in broken tones of woe which it was pathetic to listen to, 'Oh, oh, oh, my misery: oh, how can I bear such misery. Oh, my sin, my sin!

P.W.   'I have come here to help you, but what shall I call you? I cannot call you Lady Rochford now and I don't know your name. What was your Christian name?'

Lady R. 'Oh, my name; I have soiled and polluted my name. I have dragged it in the dust.'

P.W.   'But what was it?' (I am afraid that I pressed her to give her name partly for evidential reasons, as I had never heard it and I suppose it could be traced.)

Lady R. 'I cannot tell you now. I will tell you some other time. Oh, oh, do you say that you can help me?'

P.W. 'I have come to help you. I want to tell you that if you repent and turn to the Lord Jesus He can save you.'

Lady R. 'Where is Jesus? How can I see Him? How can I hear Him speak? How can such a one as I ever be forgiven. Oh, Jesus save me, save me.'

P.W. 'Jesus can speak to you through His servants. I am a clergyman, His minister and I am commissioned by Him to tell you that if you confess your sins, He is faithful and just to forgive you your sins.'

Lady R. 'Do you believe it?'

P.W. 'Yes I do believe it.'

Lady R. 'And you think I can be saved, I who have committed such a terrible sin?'

P.W. 'Why did you do it?'

Lady R. 'Oh, don't ask me. Oh, don't remind me of it. I had a child . . . . George . . . , did . . . , not , . . . believe it . . . . was . , . , his . . . . child, but it was, it was.'

P.W. 'Was it really his child?'

Lady R. 'Yes, yes, it was his child, oh, oh, oh!'

P.W. 'Did it live?'

Lady R. 'Yes it did live, Oh, oh!'

P.W. 'How can I help you. Do you know that Henry has been helped. He has repented and had been forgiven.'

Lady R. 'He treated me unjustly. He made me suffer.'

P.W. 'Yes, I know you have suffered, but Henry is sorry and he wants to undo the past, and he wants you to forgive him.'

Lady R. 'I met Henry today and Anne, and Anne took his hand and mine bloodstained both and joined them.' (Here she began weeping.)

P.W. 'What did she say?'

Lady R. 'She said: "The blood of Jesus Christ cleanseth us from all sin!".'

P.W. 'Oh, Lady Rochford it is true, believe it. The Lord Jesus has spoken to you through His Messenger and you must believe.'

Lady R. (Breaking down sobbing.) 'Jesu, whose blood cleanseth from all sin, cleanse me.'

Here she quite broke down and I myself could with difficulty restrain my own emotion and tears. There was a slight pause and silence and then as though she had pulled herself together she said quietly:

Lady R. 'Can you see me?'
P.W. 'No, I cannot see you, I am speaking to you through this lady.'
Lady R. 'That seems very strange. I am told that you have spoken to my husband and that he takes an interest in the young men's clubs in your parish.'
P.W. 'Yes, he does.'
Lady R. 'That seems very strange to me.'
P.W. 'It seems very strange to me also.'
Lady R. 'Do you see him?'
P.W. 'No, I have never seen him.'
Lady R. 'Yet, you speak to him, that seems very strange to me.'
P.W. 'Yes, it is very strange, but because it is strange it need not therefore be untrue, there are many strange things in life.'
Lady R. 'Will you speak to George for me?'
P.W. 'Yes, certainly if I get an opportunity.'
Lady R. 'Will you ask him to come and speak to me?'
P.W. 'Yes, I will, but I know that he longs to speak to you and help you. I will pray for him to come to you now.' (I then began to pray aloud.)
Lady R. (Very gently.) 'No, not that, pray him yourself to come to me, I did love him once and *I* am the mother of his child. Will you *ask* him to come and see me?'
P.W. 'Yes Lady Rochford I will.'

Then she left and we went downstairs to tea. Miss Kelly said to me: 'Will they see that I have been crying?' and I said: 'Oh, I don't think so it doesn't matter if they do.' But Maud saw it at once and my own eyes too were full of tears. It was all so pathetic and so real and again is it likely either of us would or could invent such a scene. Even to read the account of it is touching enough but to be present made one feel in the presence of a sorrow and a tragedy too lifelike to be unreal.

I have often wondered why Lady Rochford turned against her husband and brought him to the block, and jealousy of his sister the Lady Anne never seemed to me a sufficient explanation. If he believed that her child was not his child and if it really was his child, there then is much more to explain her terrible action and it would be most evidential if ever one could discover that this was the cause, but I fear the matter is too personal an affair to have had any record made in either public or private history. History so far as I can remember simply speaks of her as: 'The infamous Lady Rochford'.

CHAPTER TWENTY-FIVE

HEVER REVISITED

As my brother had asked me to pay him a visit at Eastbourne I determined to come round by Hever on my way home and wrote to ask Miss Kelly would she join Maud and myself at Lewes and come back to Sulgrave via Penshurst and Hever with us.

It was a most beautiful autumn day, Thursday, September 30th, 1926, just four and a half years since my wonderful visit to Hever Castle on January 17th, 1921.

At that time I had never met the Lady Anne and had no idea or belief that I should ever meet her, this time I was quite sure that she would be in the church ready to greet us to her old home of earth.

And so indeed it proved, for as soon as we entered the little church and were standing round the tomb of her father with its handsome and well preserved Tudor brass, and I said: 'I wonder if the Lady Anne is present,' at once Miss Kelly's pencil began to write:—

Lady Anne. 'Yes, my champion, we, Anne, her father and her brothers stand round this earthly tabernacle where lie the bones of him who was my father of earth, still united to me by the holy band of love in the grace of our Heavenly Father.'

P.W. 'Lady Anne, I want to ask you why this experience has come to me, why have I been chosen to have anything to do with the Tudor people?'

Lady Anne. 'My dear friend the reason is not far to seek; all are needed who will lend their aid in this work.'

P.W. 'Yes, but I am only one of millions, and why should I be chosen?'

Lady Anne. 'One of millions of millions, it matters not so thou
be willing to lend thine ear. We seek ever such as
can be made to hear, to see, to feel; thou knowest
not how oft it is we who impress thee, but when
thine ear is attuned to hear, then we can make the
contact we need clearer. Much work waits to be
done, the harvest is ready but the reapers few.'

This reply did not quite meet my difficulty, and two nights
later as the Lady Anne was speaking to us at Sulgrave I again
took up the subject and I shall put her fuller reply here so as to
keep it all together.

P.W.   'It seems to me that it is entirely a matter of sympathy, I was in sympathy with your misfortunes
and sorrows and so you could get into contact with
me.'

Lady Anne. 'No it is much more than that, though sympathy
plays its part.'

P.W.   'Well is it due to the family connection which I
know now exists between us?' (My brother had to
my surprise worked out our family ancestry through
the Boleyn family.)

Lady Anne. (Laughing.) 'No it is not due to pedigree. Perhaps
this will help thee to understand. If thou hast a
number of pupils, thou dost see that certain ones
among them are suited or apt for certain forms of
work, and then thou dost endeavour to impress
upon them thine ideas for them and to prepare
them specially for the work for which thou dost
know they would be fitted if only they could be
awakened and interested. Thus it was necessary in
the first place to impress and awaken thee and then
afterwards thy sympathy increased thy power of
service. Does this help to make it clearer?'

P.W.   'Yes, much clearer.'

Lady Anne. 'And now Will, wilt thou let thy mind rest and not
trouble thyself more about this matter.'
(Laughing.)

P.W.   'Yes, Lady Anne, I won't bother any more about

it, but I should tell you that the real reason why I asked so much about it was because I met a lady at Eastbourne who was very strong on reincarnation and it was suggested that this might be the explanation of it.'

Lady Anne. (Shaking her head.) 'I have never said any such thing to thee.'

P.W. 'No, Lady Anne, but it has been said to me by others also.'

Lady Anne. 'No, no, I have never made any such suggestion and it is not so.'

P.W. 'Now I am quite satisfied Lady Anne and will let the matter drop.'

This explanation of the Lady Anne puts the strangeness of my connection with these experiences upon a more probable and reasonable basis. Someone was wanted who was a possible agent both to take an interest in the Tudor period, have time and inclination to write the Play and also be likely to be led on to sympathy and prayer for Henry. The number of possible agents would be limited and the best for one reason or another might not be available, and so the choice finally fell on me. That is at least understandable and the way we work on earth. We have to employ not the best possible agents, but the best taking all the circumstances into account.

Oddly enough a short time ago Miss Kelly received a message that on the other side the Lady Anne had been chosen with a number of other prominent historical people to take part in the bringing back to earth this visible and audible contact with the unseen which Sir Oliver Lodge and others believed to be one of the great movements before our race.

If this is true then she was chosen for definite and understandable reasons and in the same way I on earth was chosen, and there for the present I must leave the problem and return to the little church at Hever.

P.W. 'Lady Anne do you remember where you sat in this church?'

Lady Anne. 'I sat not near this tomb, but further down the middle aisle on the left.'

This is rather interesting for I have always told people that she sat near the tomb in the North transept. Now I saw on this visit that in the North transept there used to be a side altar and so the Boleyn pew could not have been there.

P.W.   'Do you remember your old Vicar?' (Dr Heath.)
Lady Anne. 'My vicar stands near thee now, canst speak of aught to him thou dost wish.'

Miss Kelly then asked me if I knew anything about him and I said: 'Oh yes, I know a good deal about him; he became Archbishop of York and Chancellor and signed the writ of death for Cranmer, but the Lady Anne would not know these things as they happened after her death.'

At once to my surprise the pencil wrote and Dr Heath was speaking to me.

Dr Heath.   'Yea brother I do know thou knowest me. Speak and I will strive to answer.'
P.W.   'Do you remember the Lady Anne?'

Miss Kelly said that he seemed amazed I should ask such a question.

Dr Heath.   'How could I forget one so bound up with my prayers and my sorrows of earth?'
P.W.   'But you differed from her very widely in thought. She was progressive and reforming and you adhered to the Roman School.'
Dr Heath.   'But now I do thank the dear Lord so partnered with me in the joy of this heavenly life.'

I am afraid that I did not particularly want a long conversation with Dr Heath and as the evening was coming on and time was precious, I dropped the conversation rather abruptly and hope he will pardon me in the circumstance.

P.W.   'Lady Anne do you remember this old church?'
Lady Anne. 'Yes, not as it was in my day, but I do sense the difference through thee.'
P.W.   'How is Henry getting on. Is he progressing?' Here the Lady Anne evidently stood aside and another

hand took the pencil which wrote very slowly and unlike the former writing these words:—

'Love is guiding him along the upward, rugged path, I do thank thee all who gave me aid. Not yet am I ever with my dear love, but I do see him and I wait in patience for his fuller knowledge. I thank thee all and I am happier now.

Katherine.'

So here was the faithful Katherine and what more fitting than that the Lady Anne should stand aside and let her answer such a question herself, though it never occurred to me when I asked it, that she would do so.

I then asked the Lady Anne whose was the little slab marked with a cross just beside the large tomb of her father and she replied: 'My baby brother.'

I then turned to Maud and said: 'Shall I switch off from the church and history and ask her about Harold?' Harold is our third boy and certain ideas and plans were discussed at East-bourne about him and we felt the need of guidance. Maud however replied: 'Oh, we can leave questions about Harold until we get home.'

At once the Lady Anne wrote: 'But it is the mother's heart that draws me. I would have my champion know our interest is no way lessened. We watch and guard and when we can point out a way. I do feel thou (E.K.) canst not hear me well and had best be on the road ere night falls. I will attend again be very sure.

Anne.'

This was all indeed good advice especially that we should be on the road, for it was a quarter to five, and we had poor lights and a long run to Frensham about fifty miles along unknown and very winding roads. So we said goodbye and left the little church and reached Frensham just about seven-thirty where we stayed the night with Edith Harmar, Maud's sister.

CHAPTER TWENTY-SIX

BECKENHAM

Mrs Crawford Smith who had taken such an interest in my story from its inception, was very anxious that it should have the fullest possible confirmation and very much wished me to meet a friend of hers, Mrs Barkell who was I believe considered to be one of the finest sensitives or mediums in England. She said that she would make all the arrangements and meet all the expenses, and I could only thank her for her kindness and fall in with her plans.

I was the more anxious for some fresh or outside help because a book had just been published which stated that Mary Boleyn, the sister of the Lady Anne, was at the present time re-incarnated in the lady who wrote the book. It seemed strange that I should not have heard of such a remarkable fact if it was true, and I knew that if I could speak to the Lady Anne she would know one way or the other. Mrs Crawford Smith was so anxious that Mrs Barkell should know nothing about me that she simply told her that she was making arrangements for a friend to visit her, and did not even tell her whether it was a man or woman, and of course Mrs Barkell had never heard of me or of my Tudor story.

The day set apart for the meeting was January 4th, 1927, and as the roads were ice bound I went up to London the day before and slept with Mr Hely Smith, my friend the artist, so that I might be sure of being at Beckenham at the appointed hour. I felt that a good deal might depend on this interview as to the corroboration of my story, and I naturally therefore took it rather seriously, and as I had a quarter of an hour to spare when I reached Kent House Station, I turned into Holy Trinity Church for quiet and prayer.

Then I went to Mrs Barkell's house and found her quite ready to receive me in her warm, cosy sitting room with a small table and pencil and paper ready for me to take notes.

She said laughingly: 'I have not the least idea who you are, I only know that you are a friend of Mrs Crawford Smith and she did not even tell me whether I was to expect a gentleman or a lady.'

Then I told her that owing to the frozen state of the roads I had been obliged to sleep the night in London and had just come down by train.

'From London,' she said, 'If you had not told me you had come from London, I would have said you had come from Hampton Court or Windsor. I am a little clairvoyant, and I see these places in the background, and now I see a cross of rough wood and it is slowly turning round and showing on the other side a cross of great brightness. And I hear the name Henry connected with it and with some work which you have done in connection with him. The cross has slowly turned round from the dark side to the light and it is evidently symbolic. And now I get the word 'manuscripts', they are not ancient but modern MSS., with which you are connected.

'Now I get the name of Anne or Annie and I am conscious of the presence of a very beautiful girl. I seem to be back in Elizabethan or pre-Elizabethan times, and I seem to be in a cobbled courtyard at Hampton Court and there is a great deal of bustle and confusion. And now there is a great enclosed garden at Hampton Court and this lady is walking round it and it was a place of fear.

'Someone seems to be impressing me to see it. Now she seems going away from Henry along country lanes and I see this word written on a road post: "Send" and there is a sense of terrible fear.'

(As she spoke slowly I had time to write down all that was said word for word.)

'I do not understand this, can the lady tell me where it was?'

'She says it was where she hid for a while.'

(A few weeks previously the Lady Anne had told Mrs Crawford Smith that she wanted to give her champion a historical test which he was to search for, namely that she had been shut up in a dark room by Henry and cruelly treated. When asked whether it was in the Tower or Hampton Court she had replied 'No, no, it was a large room in a country house. My champion is to find out about it in history. I give it to him for a test.'

I thought she was now probably referring to this test, but as I knew of no such house or any such event in history, I said to Mrs B., that I knew nothing of such a hiding place, but that she had picked up the right names in Henry and Anne.)

Mrs B. replied that probably it would come out in time, and then she said very quietly: 'Come along now, White Hawk, I am getting tired.'

In a moment she was controlled by White Hawk, her Indian control of whom I had heard from Mrs Crawford Smith, and suddenly she got up and came across the room and shaking me very warmly by the hand said: 'Good morning Sir, I am White Hawk and am very pleased to meet you.'

I was naturally a bit surprised, but standing up and shaking him by the hand I said: 'Good morning, I too am very glad to meet you.'

(White Hawk then sat down again and making a large sign of the cross in the air before him said:—)

W.H. 'Is that a good sign?'
P.W. 'Yes, it is the best sign.'

(White Hawk spoke in rather broken English, but I shall relate what he said in ordinary English.)

W.H. 'What are you doing with Kings?'
P.W. 'I am trying to help a king.'
W.H. 'By the mercy of the Great Spirit and by the power of Love, you have helped a king, he is turning from darkness to light and the Lady Anne she tells me that you and she are old friends.
     (*Amazing.*)
P.W. 'I want that explained. How are we old friends?'
W.H. 'You know each other in the spirit. She is showing me gold links; you are linked together in spirit.'
P.W. 'Does she know anything about my being a reincarnation of her brother.' (A statement supposed to be made by Henry in the book mentioned.)

W.H. 'You are linked in spirit in the heavenly world and you meet her in the heavenly world and in your sleep at night. Did you not dream lately of a garden?'

P.W. 'Yes, I had an extraordinary dream about a garden.' (I had told no one of this.)

W.H. 'You met her then in sleep in that garden. I do not see the links of reincarnation here. No, I cannot see such links. I touch the spirit of the Lady Anne and I touch the spirit of purity, but when I touch big man (Henry) it is different. He has changed much but there is still much to change and he is not quite trustworthy. He has not quite lost his arrogant spirit and he must needs be purged.'

P.W. 'Does she believe that her sister is reincarnated now on earth?'

W.H. 'She says: "No, no," she is most emphatic about it and says that she cannot countenance the idea. She says: "How can Mary be incarnate in a body of flesh, when she is now with me in spirit?" And she also says that knowing Henry as well as they do, how could they rely on his word, since he has not yet reached that state or purity which is needed and which will take years of toil. She says again that she cannot countenance the idea and says do you think if this was so, she would have left you unaware of it all this time.'

P.W. 'No, I did not think she would.'

W.H. 'The Lady Anne has a pretty laugh. She is laughing now and says: "Do not believe in this half and half business". Now there is a Lady Katherine here and she says that this is but another proof that the whole of his deceiving nature is not purged, and that he has the cunning to lead others astray. Lady Katherine says that you have helped her very much. She seems to have been a very sad lady, but you have helped her into a broader light. Poor lady, poor lady!'

P.W. 'Tell her I am glad if I have helped her.'

W.H. 'Now there are lots of people crowding in. Who is Jane? She seems only a girl. The Lady Anne is putting her arms around her in friendship. The lady has brought her here and she is doing this to show you her love for her.

Katherine is also standing in the group and Parr, who is
Parr? (Katherine Parr, the sixth wife.) What are they all
doing here?

Now the Lady Anne speaks and answers, "What women
always do, giving of our love and wisdom and understanding that we may take one soul back".'

P.W. 'What soul?'

W.H. 'Henry's. White Hawk now sees Henry standing apart
and gloating. Katherine says there are two Henrys.'

P.W. 'I know, it is a sign to me connected with her.'

W.H. 'Can you not get on with writing from her?'

P.W. 'No, she seems quite unable to impress me in these ways
of sight, hearing or automatic writing.'

W.H. 'She says that she impresses your mind.'

P.W. 'Will you ask her to tell me something about her brother
George.'

W.H. 'Why does he wear a red robe? George has been healing
and the colour is for healing vibration. You will find a
mission of healing power in yourself by anointing with oil
thus. (Here White Hawk made the sign of the cross on his
forehead, throat and centre of body) and it should be
done in the name of the Master Jesus and with prayer.
Would you like to hear White Hawk's prayer for healing?'

P.W. 'Yes, very much indeed.'

W.H. 'Oh, Thou loving and Holy Lord Jesus, Thou Who givest
to Thy people power to heal the sick and to cast out evil,
we ask Thee to lay Thy healing hands upon this Thy
child, casting out his sickness and bringing in strength
and healing. Even so, come now, O Lord. Did you follow
it?'

P.W. 'Yes, but I could not get all the words down, still I got the
gist of the prayer.'

W.H. 'Oh, that is sufficient. Call on Him to lay His healing
hands upon the sick and to give you perfect faith.'

P.W. 'I have been told this before and I have tried and I have
not been successful; at least not in some cases and it has
shaken my confidence.'

W.H. 'Your failure is due to want of faith. Don't you remember
how even the Master Himself could do no mighty works

because of unbelief. Ask Him to increase your faith, for the healing power is with you. Now another has come. He says it is Wolsey. He is a sad figure and was arrogant also in his earthly life. He says that you have helped him.'

P.W. 'How have I helped him?'

W.H. 'He says by a humble faith that draws us all to the fountain of goodness. He comes because of the work of shepherding the sheep. (Do you call it?) Why does he call you Welsh – Walsh?'

P.W. 'Because it is my name.'

W.H. 'Now he is showing me a package. Packing, packing. He is trying to show me your name. Packing, packing – I cannot get it.'

P.W. 'It doesn't matter. Shall I tell you my name?'

W.H. 'No, let him try. Packing – packing . . . . packing bacon – now I can see it.'

P.W. 'Well you have nearly got it: it should be Packingham. Packingham' (laughing).

W.H. 'The Lady Anne is laughing at White Hawk, she has a very pretty laugh and even the stern looking man (Wolsey) has a smile round the eye.'

P.W. 'I don't wonder. I am very glad to know that they have such a sense of humour on the other side of the veil.'

W.H. 'The Lady Anne says that you have a sense of humour too. She says that she sees it when you visit an old lady: she goes with you and sees the sense of humour inside.'

P.W. 'Is it an old lady in the parish?'

W.H. 'Yes, she has a bad chest and coughs like this.' (Amazing – it was an old woman, Mrs Goffe, who often talks to me of 'Hannah Bullen' and ''Enery' and when she coughs says 'You'll excuse me, Sir'.)

P.W. 'White Hawk, I want to ask you why is all this taking place at the present time; this rescue work for the Tudor people and all this increase in psychic powers, the increasing communication between the seen and the unseen. Has it any special significance and what is it all leading up to?'

W.H. 'Now is the time when people must come to the knowledge of the truth. What you see all around you, these present floods, the storms, the earthquakes are all signs of the times and what you see taking place in the spiritual world is an awakening to the realities of the unseen and the importance of the spiritual life. There is going to be a time of much trouble, earthquakes and storms and confusion, but England will be greatly sheltered. Over it God has put His hand and nothing of great tribulation will be allowed to touch it. I see a hand spread all over the word as a dark shadow with the little finger on England, and under this small finger is a torch of light. It is the light of God's love to redeem all mankind. Every two thousand years there is a manifestation of the Great Spirit. "The day of the manifestation is at hand." During the next ten years there will be a wonderful outpouring of the Spirit of God and then there will come a regenerated world and then the hidden will be revealed and the unseen will be visible and you will yourself speak with the Lady Anne.'

P.W. 'But I won't be alive in ten years time.'

W.H. 'Rubbish.' (True January 1958 over 30 years later.)

P.W. 'Do you mean that all the people on earth will be able to speak to those beyond the veil?'

W.H. 'No, the spiritually minded on both sides will come together. All that is taking place now is preparation for this and the Lady Anne has been leading you up to the knowledge of these things.'

P.W. 'Does the Lady Anne wish this to be made known? She said before that my story was not to be published.'

W.H. 'The Lady Anne says that soon things may be so changed that the story may be made public. She is not sure but she thinks so. The Lady Anne again says that she has explained the principal thing for which she came and she wishes once more to emphasise to you what she has already stated, that there is no link by reincarnation between you, nor is her sister Mary reincarnated. The link between you is only in spirit. Now, I must return and go home.'

Mrs Barkell did not alter in any way: she just put her hands to her eyes and rubbed them as though she were awakening from sleep, though her eyes had never been closed. She was quite unconscious of all that had been said and so I could only tell her that Mrs Crawford Smith's kindness had been rewarded for the meeting had brought me into touch with those I sought. She said that she was very pleased and so we said goodbye. There are only three possible solutions in my mind for such a wonderful experience.

Mrs Crawford Smith might have been in league to deceive me and both be thoroughly deceitful women, which I know they were not.

Or I had actually again spoken with the Lady Anne and she had solved my problem.

Or somehow or other Mrs Barkell had picked the names—Henry, Anne, Katherine, Wolsey out of my mind.

This last possibility of telepathy would be shattered if only I could unravel the test which the Lady Anne had given, for no such house or incident had ever been in my mind, nor is it mentioned in any history, and so to this test I must devote a separate chapter.

CHAPTER TWENTY-SEVEN

SEND

'I see this word written on a road post *Send* and there is a sense of terrible fear,' this was what Mrs Barkell saw and felt when I visited her in the January of 1927.

The word Send was evidently connected with the historical test given me by the Lady Anne and meant to help me to find some house in a room of which she had been shut up and cruelly treated by Henry.

She could not remember where it was, the word did not help me for I naturally took it for a verb, and I imagined that the Lady Anne intended me to understand that in her fear and misery she wanted to send some message or messenger or wanted help sent probably by her sister Mary.

I had found out many of the tests given by the Lady Anne, but this one appeared to me so difficult, and the word Send so meaningless as a clue, that I did not perhaps study it as carefully as I should have, and soon gave it up as unsolvable.

And so I laid the whole matter aside thinking that the Lady Anne had given a test which was incapable of solution, and more than a year passed by.

Then suddenly in a most unexpected manner the key to the riddle was put into my hands. My sister Mary, in whose house at Canford Cliffs, Bournemouth, the Lady Anne had first manifested herself, invited me to stay for a few days with her and I motored down to her from Sulgrave on June 18th, 1929, little imagining what was in store for me.

After tea I was reading about my interview with Mrs Barkell and when I came to the words: 'I see this word written on a road post, Send,' I paused and said: 'I have no idea what this means, but I suppose in her trouble she wanted to send a message for help.'

Quietly and little realising how much it meant, a lady, Mrs Napier-Clavering, who was also staying with my sister said: 'But Send is the name of a place and it is quite close to us in Surrey.'

I stopped reading for it suddenly dawned upon me that I probably had the key put into my hands and that the house which the Lady Anne wanted me to find was near a place called Send, and that Send was quite close to the home of the lady before me.

My astonishment, I am told, was visible in my face, and no wonder, though Mrs Napier-Clavering knew of no old Tudor house in her neighbourhood, but she suggested that I should investigate for myself and very kindly gave me an invitation to stay with her at Chobham the following week.

Would there be a Tudor house near Send and would I be able to enter it, and if I did enter would it be possible to discover whether the Lady Anne had ever been there, and more difficult still to find out whether she had ever been shut up there and cruelly treated by Henry. These were the questions revolving in my mind, and I could see no way in which they could be completely answered, for minute details of history such as this are not generally recorded in any history book.

It was Tuesday, July 2nd, 1929, a year and a half after the test had been given, that I visited Chobham and after lunch set out with Mr Napier-Clavering to search for a Tudor house, which in the meantime he had found mentioned in a local guide to Woking and of which the modern name was Sutton Place.

We passed through Woking and then I saw to my great satisfaction a road post on which was the key word Send, and soon after we reached the gate to Sutton Place.

Fortunately, as we say, there was a lady standing at the entrance who was able to tell us exactly what to do. She said that the agent's cottage was in the fields about half a mile up the drive and that our best plan would be to go straight to him and make enquiries.

So we drove up the fine winding avenue, past a little chapel and then left the car and went down a side path to the agent's cottage.

The agent, Mr Kerr, was out but his assistant asked us to

return in an hour's time which we did. Mr Kerr told us that the
Duke of Sutherland to whom Sutton Place belonged was coming
into residence that very evening, but that if I wrote a letter, he
would give it to the Duke and he was quite sure that later on
when the house was empty I could get permission to see over it.
He did not know of any visit of Queen Anne Boleyn to the house,
though Queen Elizabeth had certainly been there, but he promised to borrow for me a book called: *Annals of an old Tudor
House,* by Frederick Harrison, which I could study when I
came.

It proved to be most fortunate and indeed essential to the un-
ravelling of the test that the Duke was coming into residence that
day, for had the house been empty and the agent immediately
shown me over it, I should have missed all that I shall now
relate.

When Mrs Napier-Clavering heard that the house had been
discovered and that I should be able to see over it, she very
kindly suggested that Miss Kelly should come and stay with
her so that we could go over the place together.

Permission to visit the house arrived in due time, and it was
arranged with the agent to go there on August 13th and he gave
the housekeeper notice that we should be coming.

Mrs Marriott, who has already come into my story, invited
us both to stay with her at Hartfield, Sussex, for August 12th, so
as to give the Lady Anne an opportunity of coming and giving
us any message or directions.

It was a very happy evening in a most beautiful spot, with
trees and bracken all about and Ashdown forest filling up the
background, and I felt sure that the Lady Anne would come,
nor was I mistaken for immediately after supper she came
through Miss Kelly and said: 'Tell my champion – Henry, Mary,
Elizabeth, George are all here.'

Then Miss Kelly said: 'She has a white veil over her face and
now she is taking it and turning it back, it is a symbol of the
long silence of a year and a half since the test had been
given.'

Then the Lady Anne said: 'You are hot upon the scent and
when you reach the room, then I will come to you.'

Miss Kelly then saw her drawing Henry by the hand, and she

said again that when we reached the right room she would bring Henry with her and so indicate it.

(I was naturally a bit excited and said:)

P.W. 'Then we have got it, we have found the right room.'

Lady Anne. (Laughing.) 'It is the right house but you have not yet found the right room.'

Then Miss Kelly saw Mary Boleyn lay her hand on my shoulder and say to her sister: 'Now make me known to him.'

It will be remembered that at Mrs Barkell's the Lady Anne had promised to bring her sister to me to prove that there was no reincarnation of her now on earth.

Lady Anne. 'Mary, this is my champion, and these are my friends, and this (a Mr Coffin), I hope will be my friend, and now my champion will you speak to my sister.'

P.W. 'Lady Mary.'

M. Boleyn. 'Not Lady.'

P.W. 'What shall I call you then; may I call you Mary?'

M. Boleyn. 'Yes, just Mary.'

P.W. 'Well, Mary, your sister says that you were connected with Send, what was the connection?'

M. Boleyn. 'That is what you have to find out – I must not solve my sister's puzzle.'

Mary Boleyn then said that she had lived in the house we were to visit before the period of her sister's sorrow and that there was a connection between the house and her first marriage. 'You will be able to trace it, but not with ease.'

Then Lady Mary Boleyn made way for her sister.

Lady Anne. 'Bid my champion listen. I wish him to remember *all* I said at our last interview.'

She then passed over to me a little pointer which Miss Kelly was using and said to me very slowly and distinctly:—

Lady Anne. 'Look at it. It is a casket, a heart. Fill it, but do not shut it down. Leave it room to overflow. Henry hath need of the overflow, much need. My champion thou hast held angry thoughts; these help not.'

I looked at the marker, which was a silver heart about the size of a hen's egg and opened like a locket. It was to be filled with love and not shut down so that some love might overflow for Henry. I felt the gentle rebuke, for candidly when Henry had begun talking about a double personality and reincarnation, etc., as related in the book before referred to, I had begun to lose interest in him and even to question the validity of my whole story.

Now the Lady Anne shows she is conscious of all this and that such an attitude of mind is not helpful and that Henry still needs love and prayer, and next Sunday at the altar I remembered the casket symbol and prayed that I might have a heart more filled with love.

P.W.   'Lady Anne, may I ask about Lady Rochford. How is she getting on?'
Lady Anne. 'She is making progress slowly.'

Then E.K. saw a child who was helping her, probably the child over which the trouble had arisen.

Lady Anne. 'Your visit to Send has taken much planning on our side to bring about, but now I will be with you when you reach the house and will indicate the right room.'
P.W.   'The agent says he is arranging for the housekeeper to show us round, could you not manage to get her out of the way?'
Lady Anne. (Laughing!) 'That is your province rather than mine.'

Next day, August 13th, I drove Miss Kelly to Chobham where we had lunch with the Napier-Claverings and then we both set out for Sutton Place and soon we were knocking at the door.

I had found out a little more about the house and that it had been built by Sir Francis Weston whose son and heir had been put to death with Henry Norris and others in connection with the Lady Anne, but I could not find out whether she had ever been there, though the Woking guide stated that in the windows of the Great Hall there were her armorial bearings, the Falcon and Tower.

The door was opened by the kindly, well nurtured housekeeper who suggested that after we had seen the house we
might study the Annals, which the agent had left for us, but she
insisted on showing us round and we were helpless.

I shall not attempt to describe the house in detail. We saw the
actual tables and chairs used in Henry's time, but Miss Kelly
made no sign except that at the top of the great stairs when
entering the long gallery she asked the housekeeper was there
no room leading off it. She replied that originally the gallery
had been a chapel with a room behind it, now all thrown into
one.

We came downstairs and I thought the whole expedition had
been a failure, when on the withdrawal of the housekeeper,
Miss Kelly told me of her experience which later on she wrote
down and which I now copy.

'Just as we reached the top of the stairs I had a sense of overwhelming terror and of being brutally dragged along by one
arm by a huge and very strong man. The feeling of helplessness
and terror was horrible. I of course thought there must be a room
opening off the gallery at the far end and asked the housekeeper about it and she explained that originally there had been
one.'

We sat down at the table where the Annals lay open and I
was explaining that there must have been a passage to the right
of the chapel to the room behind it, along which E.K. felt herself dragged, when at once her pencil began to write:

'My champion is right. Here was I dragged with cruel force,
which bruised and nigh broke my slender arm by Henry. Here
today he walketh with me sorrowful and tender. Forgiven is all
wrong but not yet forgotten. The broken vessel must be mended
ere again it can contain the wine. Mary my sister, came nigh to
death in this house and for me, my heart was broken within its
prison walls. I lay a prisoner and knew my end was near. Oh,
that I had known the hope of this dear time to follow, this light
of heavenly love and understanding that maketh of the past but
a stepping stone to Heaven's peace. Ask of my champion
patience, hope and courage. We watch and guide.'

Here the writing stopped. I suppose she had finished all that
was necessary. We had found the room and deciphered the test

and I said: 'Then I was right; she was shut up in that room early in 1536 after the birth of her child.'

Slowly the pencil wrote again: 'The *death* of my child.' For of course it was still-born.

I had often wondered what had happened to her in those few months early in 1536 before she died. Her son still-born in January meant that she was doomed, and what more natural than to flee to the friendly home of the Westons and then to be locked up there by Henry while the plots were laid to encompass her death. The fact that she fled to that house would confirm Henry in his suspicion of young Weston who was also put to death, although his mother came in person to plead for him, throwing herself at Henry's feet.

It all seemed to hang together, but would the Annals throw any more light upon it. Had the Lady Anne ever been in the house to make it likely for her to flee to her friends in her trouble.

Yes, there it was, the record of a visit which she made immediately after her coronation in 1533, and also the statement that the Westons were among the few leading families who heartily welcomed her marriage with Henry, who knighted Francis on the occasion.

How very wonderful it seemed and we spent that evening with the Napier-Claverings telling them of our adventures and of our success.

Truly I felt that the truth of my story had gained a fresh and undeniable confirmation, for on no theory of telepathy could I have been told of a house of which I had never heard and unravelled a mystery of which no history has kept a record.

CHAPTER TWENTY-EIGHT

THE OPEN WINDOW

ST JOHN THE BAPTIST'S DAY, JUNE 24th, 1933
MY LAST MEETING WITH THE TUDORS

After a couple of years of silence I had an invitation to meet a Mrs Heber-Percy in London who was a friend of Mrs Monson and has not only clairvoyant gifts but also does very remarkable inspirational paintings. She is a direct descendant of the old Percy family of Northumberland and also of Bishop Heber of India who wrote: *From Greenland's Icy Mountains.*

On the evening before we were to meet, the Lady Anne came to Mrs Monson and wrote the following:

Lady Anne. 'Yes, write Theo, it will come easily, I have that I would dictate to thee before thou meetest my Champion tomorrow. Listen:—

> There is a jewel fair
> Men know it not and pass it by,
> Pass by that Precious Stone, which hidden lies
> Yet not so deeply but that those who seek
> May surely find, do they but earnestly
>   endeavour so to do.
> And yet, alas daily men tread with heavy foot
> Upon its purity, and even spurn it from them
> Roughly, so blind are they,
> Blinded by earthly mire, that clings and clogs
> Impeding their steps, dragging them ever downwards
> Down to the depths, where no faint glimmer
> Of that Jewel shines,
> Unless, perchance, some innocent and loving soul

Untouched, untainted by earth's mire,
Hearing those stumbling steps and muttered oaths,
With purest faith, thinking no evil
May follow after such poor, erring ones,
When, as they follow Love's intent
Behold from out its hidden place
Through all that fog of earth
The precious jewel shineth forth
Its rosy light illumining their path,
That they the way may clearly see
The way Love paints.
E'en to the darkness of despair and crime
    and evil deeds, Love shineth
When the pure in heart go forth to seek and save.

> That is all tonight friend Theo, save that George and I would fain seek for entrance to the garden of the healing friend whom thou callest Wendy (Mrs Heber-Percy): we would converse with thee both, and friend Will, in the room that openeth upon her garden. Though in a busy city it remindeth me of when I tended a garden.'

Again, as ever the Lady Anne's message is couched in language chaste and poetical, and to her mind pure and unselfish Love is the precious jewel which lightens up the pathway of the soul-seekers and finally wins its entrance and finds a response in the depths of despair.

So as soon as we reached the house and Mrs M. had read the message, we went into a room with a French-window opening on a beautifully kept garden.

It was extraordinarily quiet and restful for a London garden, and bore the marks of constant care and love, having a little aviary at the end, in which were many kinds of birds, both home and foreign, some of them actually building their nests as we watched them.

We sat in chairs facing the quiet garden, and Mrs H.-P. asked me would I ask God's blessing in prayer upon the home and our meeting.

Then almost at once Mrs M. saw the Lady Anne and Mary Wyatt and George Boleyn, and many other Tudor people coming into the garden, which was flooded with sunlight, and they all greeted us in unison saying: 'We want to greet our new friend and hostess.' This, of course, was Mrs Percy.

Then the Lady Anne came forward all in white, and said: 'I want to greet my champion, my hostess and you Theo; though my friend will perhaps know it not, I am often with him in his own garden. I have tried to bring many here today; all is so peaceful so helpful that words should come easily.'

Here Mrs Monson saw George Boleyn coming across and standing beside me, and Mary Wyatt coming forward saying:

Mary Wyatt. 'I will make sweet music when thou hast thy wonder organ. There is one thou must see who will both advise and help thee that thou hast the best materials.'

I had not been thinking or speaking of the 'Wonder Organ', but Mary Wyatt is evidently quite aware that a gift of £300 had just been made to me from America with which to purchase an organ for Sulgrave Church, and I had just secured from Claypole of Peterborough an organ which Mr St George Moore said was worth quite £500. He is no doubt the 'one' who was to help and advise me.

It all shows the great interest which these Tudor friends take in the parish, and again brings out what we find so difficult to realise or believe, the practical working out of the Communion of Saints.

Mary Wyatt. 'But still friend Will has somewhat more to ask.'

P.W. 'I want to ask about Lady Rochford, how is she getting on, I have heard nothing for so long.'

Mary Wyatt. 'She is much happier and looking after children. She may be here. . . .

There was a slight pause, and then T.M. saw Lady Rochford coming forward and caught the name 'Frances'. It may be remembered that when I met her, some years before in such terrible anguish of spirit, I asked her to give me her name, rather I fear as a test. Now she gives it apparently, while I on my part have forgotten her name, if I ever knew it.

(Later, I find it was Frances–Lady Frances Vere, daughter of Lord Morley. I may have known it when I wrote the Play, but T.M. did not know it.)

Well she came forward leading a little child to me which looked up at me and smiled, and then another and another until T.M. saw children standing all round my knees.

Lady Rochford. 'That's my work. They do not mind how evil my past has been. Their kisses bring me comfort and forgetfulness. Thank this friend Anne's champion for his prayers, which have found an echo here. The little ones are often near him, I bring them to his Church and . . . .'

She broke off in the middle of her sentence, and the Lady Anne said suddenly, and as if a little surprised: 'Will, here is Henry.'

But how wonderful if it is indeed all true that Lady Rochford has been won out of her terrible misery and despair, and that my poor prayers have helped her. It was a great surprise to me that she should be there herself to thank me and a great joy to know that she was finding comfort and forgetfulness in tending and caring for children, and a thought too marvellous and solemnising I fear for my faith that she should bring them into my little church. Are the worlds really so close and interdependent as all that? What great problems her statement raises and shall we ever be given sufficient light on these mysteries as to enable us really to say we believe them. Well there was no time then for such thoughts or cogitations, for Henry Rex demanded my attention.

Henry. 'I know not this woman (Mrs Heber-Percy) does she bid me welcome?'
Mrs H.-P. 'Yes, certainly, I am very pleased to welcome you.'
Henry. ''Tis well. She hath an air that makes me feel at home. Methinks I know someone akin to her long since passed over.

(No doubt young Lord Percy, engaged to the Lady Anne.)

'Lady doth it irk thee to receive me? I am only
Henry, no king. . . . . 'Tis a peaceful spot. . . . Friend
Will, didst know I wished to see thee?'

P.W.   'No.'

T.M.   'What did you want to see him for?'

Henry.   (Thinking and frowning.) 'A Message I sent to this
         woman (T.M.) was lost.'

P.W.   'Was it about the histories which represent thee as
         wicked?'

Henry.   'It might be possible to change them.'

T.M.   'I don't think that would be possible.'

Henry.   'That is not true. If one repents why should not
         people know I am sorry. Am I ever, ever to suffer
         this remorse, never to feel that my repentance is
         known. Friend Will, what sayest thou?'

P.W.   'I am afraid Henry, that nothing can change the
         records of the past.'

Henry.   'I know I was wicked, but I would that the children
         should know I am sorry if it be possible.

P.W.   'I am afraid it would be most difficult to persuade
         people of your repentance. They would not believe
         this story of mine even if it were made public.'

Mrs P.   'In time perhaps you might be able from your side to
         impress it upon the teachers.'

Henry.   'There is much in what thou sayest friend Will, but
         methinks that what the woman there sayeth has some-
         thing in it and in time it will come. I am thankful that
         thou didst not see me in that wretched picture (*The
         Private Life of Henry VIII*, to which I was advised
         not to go); but 'twould be great if I could come
         and play a part in such a Play for those whose eyes
         could see. Friend Will, what thinkest thou of my
         message?'

P.W.   'What message?'

Henry.   'My desire to be recorded as repentant not only in
         the manuscript but that all should know, that the
         children should know; this have I said to thee before,
         but I know not how it should be done.'

P.W.   'That's the trouble! Can you suggest a way?'

Henry.   'I spake yestereen to one who was a playwright in my time. He had a strange idea which I think could be brought to pass, that if a Play could be written, a play of modern times showing the trials of this present day, if such a Play were written it would include such characters from the past as myself, Elizabeth my daughter and others, I cannot name them all now, who would return and act as would seem best to them for the good of England. Nay friend Will, I fear I am somewhat confused but perchance canst read my meaning. Have they no pity, when a man has gone before his Maker, hath watered his couch with the bitterest tears that ever flowed from men's eyes; is it of no avail to repent; must the foul echo of one's misdeeds follow for ever the repentant spirit; is my purgatory to last for all eternity?

''Tis not the truth they tell, 'tis false, adding fuel to the fire of lies over which the tongues of ages gloat and lick their lips. I command thee, nay forgive, I beseech thee give heed to my request, let there be some record made that those who come after shall read and know that Henry, once King of England did repent.

'Foul we may have been in my day, and I myself the worst sinner of my reign, but how much better are those now who gloat over the excesses, the sensualities and drunken orgies of a bygone day. Methinks thy boasted civilisation hath no cause to vaunt itself, who didst still send forth thy sons to the slaughter, to a greater bloodshed than ever stained the annals of my reign. In all these years since Henry reigned, hast thou still to learn to love thy neighbour as thyself.'

Katherine. 'Oh dear, my Lord, be calmer, let not what thou hast seen so disturb thy spirit. Knowest thou not that those bitter tears of anguish thou didst shed have washed away the stain of sin from thy garments in the Blood of the Lamb.

'See here are we all, sisters together in one deep repentance for our many and grievous misdeeds, ready

by our link of love and pity for our earthly sisters to
serve thee in thy work of restitution. Speak on
Henry, and tell friend Theo what thou wouldst have
recorded by friend Will in the Record he is making
of the Tudor ones on this side.'

Then T.M. saw all his queens gathering round him with
Mary Wyatt, Wolsey, Sir Henry Norris, Sir Thomas Boleyn,
Sir Thomas More, Cranmer and many others.

Henry.   (Much calmer.) 'My friends, this message is to all
who have helped and understood me and who will,
God willing, continue to do so, and to further the
cause we have in hand. Surely this group of those to
whom I, as King and man was both cruel and unfaithful is of itself sufficient proof that my repentance
is no vain boast. There was a day (his voice grew
low, his eyes on the ground), when these now gathered closely round me, shrank with horror and flew
terrified at my approach, so strongly did my evil
deeds still – I must use the words – stink in their
nostrils. And now, (he looked up), by the mercy of
God, the King of Heaven, the gentle Shepherd of
His Sheep, Who hung upon the cross like a common
felon for such as I – now, as Katherine said, my
tears of anguish have washed the stains of sin from
my robes.

'A while ago I was enraged, torn with distress at
what I had been taken to see, that horrible picture of
my past – in imagery drawn from the brains of men
who can never have believed in the Life to come or
in a Divine Saviour.

''Tis my punishment – I accept it – to see these
ghosts out of the past, my sinful past, but as I grow
stronger in the knowledge and understanding of the
Love of God, in the Light of Whose Countenance
we dwell, I shall learn my lesson and strive to win
back other souls to the Love and Mercy of Christ –
souls who have erred in like manner as myself. My
request to thee, Theo, to Will, to Eleanor is that

the world may know of my sorrow and of this message.'

As Henry spoke to me so earnestly the thought came into my mind that while his idea of a Play might be impossible, some day if my Tudor experiences were published his desire might be fulfilled in perhaps a more effective way.

Then suddenly Henry said: 'Friend Will, how dost fare with thee and thy wife Maud?'

P.W.   'Very much better, thank you, Maud is very well now.'

Henry.   ''Tis well, for thou hast passed through much sorrow and my heart has known and been with thee.

(He refers to Maud's almost fatal illness and the death of our eldest boy Willy in the spring of 1932, who comes into the earlier part of the story.)

'Methinks 'twould have been a holy thing to have had such sorrow . . . .'(He broke off, and to my intense joy Willy was speaking—)

Willy.   'Dad, Dad! I have been here all the time, but could not speak before being under orders. Do you know there are simply heaps of us here today, the room is crowded and such dresses! I want to say so much but it's difficult because I know you'd rather be alone with me . . . .'

This closed the interview with Henry Rex.

T.M.   'Lady Anne I would like to ask thee something. I would like to know the purpose of the manuscript, is it simply to help Henry or has it some further meaning, something more to which it is leading up?'

The Lady Anne instead of replying in words, stooped down and picked up one of the tiny yellow flowers in the garden and held it up. As she held it, it grew larger and larger until it was a great big flower, and then long tendrils reached from it outwards and upwards.

T.M.   'Is that a symbol of the MSS., leading on to greater things?'

Lady Anne. 'The manuscript is one of the ladders from here to you and from you to us, by which many may climb to true knowledge.'

T.M. then heard a voice calling 'Father, father . . . .' I thought it must be some Tudor person, perhaps that the Lady Anne's father was coming but T.M. described a tall girl advancing with brown eyes and auburn hair tinted with gold, and said: 'I believe it is your little girl,' and the next moment Helen was speaking so rapidly that I could hardly write at the pace she went, just making rough notes which I filled in afterwards.

Helen. 'Daddy, I do like this garden. I love it, Daddy I think you get lots of help here.'

This ought to encourage those who dwell in large cities and can only possess very small gardens with probably walls all round, as this little plot had. To these spirits from the higher life, size, costliness or the rareness of the flowers is not what seems to matter, but the atmosphere created by loving care, and the making the best use of the little one has. Both the Lady Anne and now Helen felt at once that this little garden in London was helpful and peaceful and Helen says: 'Daddy I love it.'

Helen. (Continuing.) 'I wish you'd tell girls more, they understand much better than boys. I mean about these spiritual things and this life. When I look back before I came over I used to think it was fairies; it was fairies in a way, but it was sent by those who are here. If we see fairies we see those here. Couldn't you write some fairy stories, Daddy?'

P.W. 'I don't think I could Helen.'

Helen. 'I will help you. I think I could when you are in the garden. Our rose garden has miles and miles of lovely roses. That's where they put the children; it is the children's summerland. Now I am very busy Daddy because I am one of the elder girls and I teach them music. I want you to tell Lilian about it.'

She had gone before I had the time or wit to ask her half a dozen questions—how could she 'think it was fairies' or anything else since she was only three months old.

When Helen had vanished, T.M. saw Queen Elizabeth very

stately, dressed in her royal robes and T.M. asked her why she
came so regally attired.

Elizabeth. 'I have not been here before and I wish to do my
hostess honour. Once near here was a beautiful
ground where I did ride. I hunted near here, so did
Henry.'

(I had no idea of this, but was told that not far off at Notting
Hill there was a royal hunting park.)

T.M. 'Have you any special message for Anne's
champion?'
Elizabeth. (Thinking.) 'I like his poetry. He will write more. I
like the way he rules his people; I mean not a kingdom. I would send a message to his lady wife –
"Had I been as good a woman as she, I had been a
better Queen".'

(When I returned home and gave Maud this message, Herbert
who was standing by said: 'Dad, I should have told Queen
Elizabeth it was stale news'.)
When Queen Elizabeth had given her message, her mother
again spoke.

Lady Anne. 'I think time fails, that which you call time – and
there is much we would have said. We greet you
all. We are much with friend Will. We would
come here again. Now we must go. We would our
champion say some word of prayer to bless us as
we bless you.'

I hesitated. Was I a poor unworthy earthly padre to pronounce a blessing in the presence of and over those from higher
worlds, and so I said: 'Does she mean that I am to pronounce a
blessing and to pray?'

T.M. 'Yes, she asks you to.'

And so I prayed:—

P.W. 'May the blessing of God our Heavenly Father, the love
of Christ our Saviour, and the Communion and inspira-

tion of the Holy Spirit rest upon us now and as we go back to our work, so that we may each of us in our own sphere be enabled to do God's holy will for us and be a help and blessing to all those with whom in His providence we may be brought into contact.'

After a short silence, T.M. saw the Lady Anne and her Tudor friends, raising up their hands in blessing and rising from the little garden.

CHAPTER TWENTY-NINE

DANAHAN

THE LADY ANNE'S MAID

After a silence of twenty years I am again called in a very remarkable way and evidently at the Lady Anne's desire, to relate a story which is quite unknown to history but which must have made a very deep impression upon her and which she seems to feel should be recorded as a tribute to one of her maids of honour, who as she puts it: 'WAS DONE TO DEATH FOR MY SAKE.'

In August 1953 I was paying a visit to Mrs Campbell at Southborough only eight miles from Hever, and though she had not read the *Tudor Story* she had read *The Communion of Saints,* published in 1953, and knew of my great interest in all that had to do with the Lady Anne.

So she suggested that we should go to Hever and take with us a Miss Martin, who had some slight mediumistic powers, though she hardly expected that anything would come of the visit, as Miss Martin was rather inexperienced and of course knew nothing about me and had no historical interest.

It was on Wednesday, August 19th, 1953, that we drove to that lovely spot, and it so happened that the Vicar (Rev. D. B. Foster) was in the Church and kindly took me round.

Miss Martin, who had separated from me while we were exploring the church, was having a remarkable experience. She felt that the church was full of spirit people and among them was the Lady Anne who seemed to compel her to enter a pew on the left side of the nave. (I had told her in the car that Hever was the home of the Lady Anne in whom I took a special interest.)

Then she saw a procession moving up the aisle and gathering

round the tomb in the North transept; this was of course the tomb of Sir Thomas Boleyn of which she knew nothing.

They were not in mourning, but she knew that it was a funeral procession, and above the tomb and above the mourners she saw a figure kneeling with her hands clasped, who seemed to be the only one who was really grieving, and she felt that this must be the Lady Anne. Sir Thomas Boleyn died in 1538 and this must have been a vision or representation of his funeral. The Lady Anne had died in 1536 and therefore could not have taken part in the funeral service, but Miss Martin saw her kneeling above the others and in prayer, which is remarkable as of course she knew nothing of the dates and circumstances.

Then she saw the Lady Anne shut up in some confined place; it was winter time for the trees were bare of leaves and the rooks were flying about them, and then she seemed to be controlled by the Lady Anne and to take on her feelings of agony and grief in the Tower before she was led out to die. It was not so much the fear of death as the sense of outrage and shame that Henry could ever have imagined her guilty of being unfaithful to him and could have brought such terrible accusations against her. Miss Martin herself took on these feelings so acutely that she was quite overcome and begged the Lady Anne to release her. This is really very remarkable when it is remembered that Miss Martin knew practically nothing at all about the Lady Anne except that she had been executed and of course had never read of her trial and protestations of innocence.

When Miss Martin had regained her composure, she asked me if the Lady Anne had been imprisoned in the Tower in the winter, and I said that it was not in winter time but in May and Miss Martin then asked how it was that she saw her quite clearly confined in winter for the trees were bare of leaves.

Then I remembered that of course she had been shut up in the room at Sutton Place after the birth of her still-born child in January 1536, the room which Eleanor Kelly and I had found (see Chapter 27) and where she was probably kept till her removal to the Tower in May. All this was quite unknown to Miss Martin and seems a confirmation of what we had discovered after I got the message 'SEND'. (Chapter 27.)

I was explaining this to Miss Martin as we stood by the tomb of Sir Thomas, when suddenly she was again controlled and felt that she was being crushed to death, and that stones were being cast upon her and that her body was, as she expressed it, being 'buckled and huddled up'. The feeling was so agonising that she begged to be released as she could not bear it.

Miss Martin seemed so completely overcome by this experience – something she had never known before – that Mrs Campbell put her arms round her and held her fearing that she might fall.

When she had somewhat recovered, I suggested that as the Lady Anne was evidently in the Church, we should ask her if she could throw some light on what seemed to us such a strange occurrence.

Miss Martin was then given a pencil and piece of paper and putting the paper on the tomb, her hand was at once controlled and these words were written:—

I AM HERE ANNE. ALL WAS AS YOU SAY. MY WOMAN WAS DONE TO DEATH FOR MY SAKE.

That was all that came in writing, but Miss Martin felt that the Lady Anne did not at all approve of the way the floor of the chapel had been raised, nor of the way in which the modern organ protruded into it. Miss Martin then showed me the pew into which the Lady Anne had compelled her to enter and I then entered in myself and spent a short time in prayer.

We had been in the church for about an hour and these experiences had taken so much out of Miss Martin that Mrs Campbell felt that we should get back home as soon as possible and so we drove at once back to Southborough.

That same evening at about eight o'clock, Mr Cox, the sensitive connected with Mrs Campbell's healing centre, came in to see me. He had not been with us to Hever and had not read the *Tudor Story* and had, I believe, very little knowledge of my interest in the Lady Anne, which makes all that now follows not only of great interest but also of very remarkable evidential value.

After going under control he spoke quite slowly so that Mrs Campbell was able to take down all that he said, and there followed a long religious talk, which is not necessary to be recorded here. He then paused and asked if there were any questions which persons present wished to ask, and I said that there were three which were very much in my mind:—

(1) How is Henry getting on? Is he progressing?

Answer: 'When your part in Henry's being led to the Light had been fulfilled, it was for him only the beginning. He was conscious he had to endure some degree of redemption for the sins that were his on earth. Your work was primarily to bring him out of the shadows to a sphere where at least he would be conscious of Light, which in due time would lead him out that he might progress and evolve through Christ. For that which he has done on earth he must continue to repent until his soul has been completely cleansed and filled with love. We would say to you that now he has started, he is progressing, but bear in mind that time in spirit is not your time, and he still has much of eternity.'

When it is remembered that Mr Cox had never met me before, knew nothing whatever of my spiritual contact with Henry, and knew nothing at all about the Tudor story, and that even Mrs Campbell herself had not then read it, this reply to my question is not only astonishing, but is about as evidential as anything that can be imagined.

I then asked my second question:—

(2) Can you tell me anything about the woman who controlled Miss Martin in Hever Church?

(It must be borne in mind that Mr Cox had not been to Hever and knew nothing about what had taken place there.)

Answer: 'The woman whose spirit made herself so distressingly obvious to Miss Martin was the maid of Lady Anne, and as a maid she had her mistress's almost complete confidence in all she did. Perhaps you do not understand; when you live in court circles it is difficult to find an ear in complete sympathy and understanding, with no ambition and no desire to make use of confidences for their own ends. Lady Anne was a woman, and as such needed sympathy from one of her own kind, and also, even though not of so exalted a position, sometimes another woman's guidance. This woman was dangerous to those who had laid false charges, and the danger could only be removed by her death. She died an extremely brutal death. She was thrown living into a pit and stones caused to cascade on her. This was also her grave. Her name was *DANAHAN*.'

This name was spelled out very slowly, which was very remarkable, for in the church Miss Martin told me that she heard the woman's name but could not get it correctly. She knew that it began with Dan or Dam and that it sounded like Damaris, and I had said that the only Damaris I had ever heard of was the name of the woman mentioned as listening to St Paul when he was preaching on the Areopagas at Athens. (Acts XVII 34.)

Now the name which Miss Martin had failed to catch was spelt out very slowly and distinctly so that there could be no mistake about it, and that by or through Mr Cox who had not been to the church and had had no communication with Miss Martin, and who had heard nothing at all about the story.

In all my long Tudor story I cannot remember anything more remarkable or more evidential than the giving of this name. Why Miss Martin should have been controlled by this unknown maid of the Lady Anne seemed to me a great mystery. Such a death and such a tragedy is of course possible and perhaps even probable if she possessed knowledge which might frustrate the plans of those who were anxious to bring false charges against her mistress, but there is no such tragedy mentioned in any history that I have read, and of course the murderers would have been very careful to see that the news of it did not get abroad.

(3) Does the Lady Anne wish the Tudor story to be published, or has she anything she wishes to be done about it?

Answer: 'The Lady Anne says that she is fully aware of both the need and the potency of these volumes, but it must be published when the time is ENTIRELY PERFECT. So we (the Control) would say, you will be instructed when this is so.'

Evidently the Lady Anne considers that the entirely perfect time has not yet arrived and she is the one who must know best.

Then Mr Cox, or rather the control through Mr Cox, gave the blessing: MAY THE BLESSING OF THE DIVINE GOD ABIDE WITH THEE AND BE THY STAFF AND COMFORTER.

When I got back to Sulgrave I wrote to Mrs Campbell to ask her if she could possibly find out something more about Danahan, and especially to ask why she had been brought in such an unexpected manner to Hever Church.

On August 27th the healing circle met again and Mr Cox, under control, gave the following reply to my question:

Answer: 'Danahan was the daughter of one of the husbandmen who worked on the Boleyn estate. There was from early childhood a certain affinity between Danahan and the Lady Anne to the degree that in childhood, had the Lady Anne been permitted, they could have been very loving playmates. What more natural than that in due time Danahan was to become the Lady Anne's maid. Within the boudoir the relationship was much deeper than that of lady and maid and was one of two deep and loyal friends. We have already mentioned that they enjoyed one anothers complete confidence, that there were indeed very few of even the most intimate secrets withheld from each other. It was Anne's father at whose feet must be laid the murder of this girl, because he realised that she could and moreover possibly would reveal the full story of the treacherous accusation of the Lady Anne, and that if this was permitted, that Sir Thomas himself could have been deeply involved and if permitted to go to the full conclusion of justice in those days, might well have lost his head.

'Danahan was little else than a common, uneducated girl, but she was lifted out of and above these limitations by a sincere and one might almost say holy love for her mistress, which would have given courage to have done that which she would have known to have been right, even sacrificing her life which indeed she did.'

(At this point Miss Martin who was present said, 'I have been given that Danahan's mother died when Danahan was born and that the Lady Anne's wet nurse brought up Danahan. I also got the name Mildenhall and Sarah and a picture of her in a grey homespun dress with white coif and apron.')

Mr Cox's control continuing:—

'The reason why this story of Danahan has been revealed is because though she did not succeed in helping her Mistress, she did indeed make a full sacrifice of her life towards this end, and it is only right and fitting that this should be part of the story of the Lady Anne.

'The reason why the Lady Anne brought Danahan with her and caused Miss Martin to suffer deep distress is because that for any spirit to return once more to the earth plane, they must in effect make a full return journey in the truest and deepest sense, that they must pass back through the spheres through which they have progressed, passing into the denser atmosphere of earth, and in so doing recapitulate again the conditions which they experienced at the passing over. This is not peculiar to any one spirit, it does apply to all. It serves a purpose, since it is often a means of establishing the identity of those who come to communicate.'

(Hence another member of the circle who evidently felt that she was getting a bit out of her depth remarked: 'We could be a lot better at history lessons you know!')

Mr Cox continuing:—

'You possibly do not realise that we who have been withdrawn from the doings and history of earth for such a long time, do now feel it difficult to give you that which you ask. You must sometimes realise and also bear with us that we only function at our best in that sphere of heaven to which we have attained. There is so much dross that is shed as one progresses ever more close to the Divine Presence. Even such eminent mortal creatures as your King Henry, really now mean so little to us, but since we have learned to love all God's creatures, no matter who they be on the path of redemption, we do ask for him God's blessing and for the Light of the Master to lead his footsteps on to surer and more solid ground. We all have our work to do, we all have our mission to fulfil for the glory of God and under the guidance of our Master. We, at best, can only be conscious of the infinitude of God, but we can have no part of it. We can only attain to some part of this complete knowledge, and it is within the scope of that knowledge to strive to work His will and leave those others better qualified in various ways to work theirs.'

Here the message through Mr Cox came to an end and I was candidly puzzled to imagine for what reason Sir Thomas Boleyn should have put his daughter's maid to death.

But my own daughter Lilian did not seem to see in it any

great difficulty. One of the false accusations brought against the Lady Anne was not only that she was unfaithful to the King, but she was trying to poison him, and that she had only married him because of the pressure put upon her by her mother. There is no doubt that pressure was put upon her, as I bring out in my Play *Anne Boleyn,* and that being so, the Lady Anne would have most probably have spoken of it to her faithful and loved maid Danahan, and someone would have told Sir Thomas of the rumours that were in the air and then to save himself becoming involved, he would realise that his daughter's maid must perish.

The whole story is now buried in the past history of 400 years ago, but evidently the Lady Anne feels that the devotion and sacrifice of the maid, who was not only the friend of her childhood but her faithful servant in the royal court at Windsor, should not be forgotten in this record of her life and I therefore agree that it should be included.

*   *   *

The unexpected appearance of the Lady Anne in Hever Church after so many years, was only one of many events in the year 1953, which turned my mind once again to the idea of publishing this strange story.

I had had several requests to allow it to be published, but I shrank from the publicity it was sure to bring and also I felt that this was a question which the Lady Anne herself must decide. I had several times referred to it, but she never seemed satisfied that what she called the 'Entirely Perfect' time had come, and so I determined to wait her bidding, and I also felt that it might not be wise to have it published while I was in charge of a country parish.

But towards the close of 1953, things seemed pointing to my resignation; I had been Vicar for over thirty years, and I was just on 86 years of age, and in 1954 should have been 60 years ordained; also my daughter Lilian who was living with me with her husband and two children was leaving and I felt that I could not stay on alone and do effective work.

I consulted my Bishop who agreed that I really had no choice, but he said that he would keep me on in the diocese as a Canon

Emeritus. All this seemed leading up not only to my retirement in 1954, but also to the possibly 'entirely perfect' time for the publication.

All through the long story I felt that I had been guided in a very wonderful way, and that people with psychic gifts had been brought to me without any effort or seeking on my part, so as to make the recording of the story possible. Now all my psychic friends had passed on within the Veil and if I was to get into contact again with the Lady Anne and find out what she wished done, I should have to make an effort, and try to find someone through whom she could communicate. Again the way opened. I had published in April 1953 my little booklet entitled *The Communion of Saints,* and this brought me into contact with many new psychic friends, and one of them suggested that I should meet Mrs Estelle Roberts, a very experienced and reliable Christian sensitive, very well known in the psychic world but quite unknown to me. After much thought and prayer I wrote to her and then met her in her own home on December 19th, 1953.

E.R. (Mrs Estelle Roberts) had never heard of me and knew nothing at all about my story or the object of my visit and, it candidly seemed to me that I was making a great venture of faith. We met in the afternoon in her well lighted cosy sitting room, just as 30 years before I had sat with Mrs Clegg in my sister's room in Bournemouth, when the Lady Anne first came to me.

Almost at once E.R. said, 'I can see that you are engaged in writing, writing, writing; it seems to me some kind of historical story.' I replied that I was writing a historical story and that it was about that story that I was seeking advice.

Then E.R. said that she saw standing beside me a beautiful spirit form with her hand on my shoulder, and pouring into my lap red roses; and then without giving any name, she described the Lady Anne in her Tudor coif and pearls, and said that she was closely connected with the story which I was writing.

Then speaking very slowly and as if rather astonished E.R. went on to say that she saw the Lady standing in a very commanding position, by some great building perhaps it might be Buckingham Palace; she has brown hair and very remarkable eyes, not blue or hazel, more like violet. Then E.R. paused and said, 'Oh, but she died young . . . . there was a great tragedy . . . . she . . . . was . . . . executed.'

I said nothing and E.R. gave no name, but then she said, 'I hear the name Henry,' and then she saw the well known figure of Henry VIII beside the beautiful spirit form and she knew that it was Anne Boleyn.

So then I told E.R. that it was the Lady Anne whom I had come to meet and that what I wanted to know was whether the Lady Anne felt that the time had come for the story to be published.

At once E.R. spoke very quickly and decidedly, nodding her head emphatically, saying that the Lady Anne wished the story to be FINISHED and then published, and I understood that the Lady Anne meant by the very emphatic word 'finished' that the extra chapter about the maid Danahan should be added.

Then as a test, I asked could the Lady Anne tell me what had happened in her old church at Hever last August.

Speaking slowly and as if feeling her way, E.R. said that she saw me in Hever Church with someone who had psychic powers (Miss Martin) and that I was there told the story of a young woman who had met with a very tragic death. Here E.R. put her hands to her neck and asked me if she had been beheaded and I replied 'No, but she was put to death very cruelly and she had been a maid of the Lady Anne.'

Then as an extra and more difficult test I asked if the Lady Anne could give me her maid's name.

Names seem always difficult and even in the Church Miss Martin could not get it correctly, but said that it sounded like Damaris.

Very slowly and hesitatingly E.R. traced on the arm of her chair the capital letter D. Then there was a long pause and E.R. traced the letter A and finally N. She seemed unable to get the rest of the name and probably the Lady Anne felt that as a test she had given enough, for what other woman's name begins DAN.

In closing, the Lady Anne said, through E.R., that she was bringing me into contact with someone who could help me with the publishing and that I had already been with him twice. This was remarkable for through the booklet *The Communion of*

Saints, I had quite recently met Mr Reginald Lester (author of *In Search of the Hereafter*) and had as a matter of fact been just twice in his rooms in London, and there for the present I must leave it until I resign my parish.

CHAPTER THIRTY

THE KING'S REQUEST

I kept thinking a great deal about Henry's request that I should write another Play introducing the Tudor people, only bringing him in as a repentant and restored child of God, but I did not feel equal to writing such a Play nor did I think it would be effective.

The only way possible to bring about the King's desire was, I felt, to have the Tudor story published so that people might have time to read it quietly, study it carefully and then form their own opinions both as to the truth of the story and also as to the reality of the repentance of the King.

It was such a pathetic appeal to me personally and I felt that I was the only one who could respond to it, and yet I was not sure that the time had come for the publication of such a story, raising as it did such great psychic and religious problems.

But before my experiences closed in 1953 a great change was beginning to take place in religious and psychic thought, and to my great surprise a little book called *The Communion of Saints,* which a London vicar asked me to write, had run into five or six editions and soon after this 'The Churches' Fellowship for Psychical Study' was formed to encourage within the Churches the study of the known facts of psychic science.

Still though I had several requests, asking me to allow my story to be published I held back because during all the writing of the story I had never taken any step without what I felt to be what Abraham's servant looked upon as divine guidance. I had never consulted a sensitive; they had come to me of their own accord, or conditions had been so planned that I should meet those who possessed these clairvoyant or clairaudient gifts and I was simply the recorder of what they told me that they saw or heard and when the Lady Anne, whose story it really is, was seen and heard in my sister's room in Bournemouth, I was so taken by surprise that I found it difficult to believe it until I had tested the reality of her presence by every means in my power.

Now twenty-five years had gone by since I had last met the Tudors or been in contact with Lady Anne and I wanted very much to know whether she wished her story ever to be made public. Whether now was the 'entirely perfect' time.

All the sensitives through whom the story had been given had gone on, and it seemed as if the story might never be made public, but would pass into oblivion.

Then as the year 1958 approached bringing with it my 90th birthday, a brilliant idea came into the mind of Mrs Vivian, a member of the C.F.P.S. Council and the author of *Love Conquers Death,* and she proposed to give a birthday party for me to which she would also invite a sensitive and this should give the Lady Anne the opportunity of being present if she so desired and letting me know definitely what she wished done as to the publication of her story.

I could not refuse such a very kind and remarkable invitation and I knew that Mrs Vivian would be very careful not only to choose a good and trustworthy sensitive, but also to keep all knowledge of me and of the story secret, and so successfully were the plans made that the sensitive did not even know that a gentleman was to be present.

The party was a complete success. The Lady Anne came almost at once and having proved to us that she was the person whom we wished to meet, she at once and before I could enter on the question of the publication of the story, said quite simply and of her own accord these words.

'The book is now finished and will go to a publisher, but find the right one. The sales will be rather slow to begin with. It does not matter. There is no hurry.'

Then the sensitive closed the party saying:—

'Anne thanks you both for affording her this opportunity to come and join you, God bless you both.' She shows me a golden Crown but she says—

'The Crown I have today is an Eternal one.'

The sensitive rubbed her eyes and opened them. She knew nothing of what she had said but Mrs Vivian thanked her warmly.

EPILOGUE

And here I shall close this strange yet interesting story, for my part in it seems to have been accomplished.

Henry has not only been reached and won over to penitence and faith, but he seems to be able to take his part now with those who are seeking to redress the wrongs of those cruel times.

It must always remain to me something of a mystery – in spite of the Lady Anne's explanations – why it was that my assistance and co-operation was called in at all.

I was living in China, far away from the homes of the Tudor people and knew practically nothing about them, and none at all of the possibility of co-operation in prayer and service between those on earth and those beyond the veil. But my sympathy with the tragedy of the Lady Anne was aroused and then gradually I was led on step by step as the story relates, until by degrees the Play was written and I was brought into touch with mediums or sensitives for whom I acted really as an amenuensis or recorder, for I myself do not seem to possess the necessary psychic gifts of clairaudience or clairvoyance.

I followed, always prayerfully, what seemed to be a guidance, if I had not done so the story could never have been written, for the opportunities which then opened up would have passed by for ever, and already all my psychic friends have passed on into that fuller life which was so vividly real to them even on earth.

What a moment that must have been for them when they met the friends, friends whom they had come to know and love through their gifts of clairvoyance and clairaudience. What a reality and wider prospect it gives to our hymns:—

> 'O then what raptured greetings
> On Canaan's happy shore.'

When those separated by time like Eleanor Kelly and Mary Wyatt meet in Jerusalem the Golden.

177

I have tried to test the truth of my story in every way open to
me and I can see no other satisfactory explanation to account for
it, except the simplest one, namely that I was the recorder of
facts.

But the story, if true, throws light on many problems and
especially on the certainty of personal survival, the sureness of
judgment, the reality of Heaven and hell, the possibility of repentance after death even though it be through weeping and
wailing and gnashing of teeth, and the Communion of Saints.
And above all it teaches us the tremendous power of love, first
of all human love, for it was through the love of Katherine that
Henry was reached, and that again leads us up to the wonderful
love of God from Whom comes all human love.

Behind the salvation of the world and working for the welfare
of every human soul is the Love of God the Father, manifested
especially for this planet in the gift and sacrifice unto death of
the Lord Jesus Christ.

My story assures us that the love of God, so undying and so
powerful, is mediated and expressed in Heaven as on earth in the
face of Jesus Christ.

I shall never forget the reply of the Lady Anne to my question:
'Who is your greatest friend?' I expected her to say; 'Mary
Wyatt,' but in the blessed life all friends yield place to One,
and so she said simply and quietly: 'The Lord Jesus He is the
great Friend of all here.'

That reply, so unexpected, so beautiful and so illuminating
bears on it the hall mark of sincerity and truth, and it is in that
great encircling friendship which my story teaches, that all true
friendship should and does subsist, whether formed on earth or
in Heaven, whether in time or in eternity.

> 'For He is before all things, and by Him all things
> hold together.'
>
> Col: I. 17.

APPENDIX I

Copy of a letter from Col. R. Lester to the Rev. J. D. Pearce-Higgins.

25th February, 1956.

My dear John,

I have had what I consider a remarkable experience today, which I feel I must pass on to you for your records. You have read the Pakenham-Walsh Tudor story, I believe, so will know all about Anne Boleyn.

As you know, I rarely have sittings these days – about two a year at most, just on special occasions. I had tried to arrange a sitting this week with a certain medium at M.S.A., but she was taken ill and I had to have a Scottish medium named Mrs Jean Thompson – a complete stranger to me, as I was to her. I went along expecting nothing more than an average sitting.

At the start of the sitting my first wife came through with some quite good evidence, and then my mother. Then, as you will see from the first of the attached extracts, they both stepped aside to allow another lady to come through, whose name conveyed nothing to me, and whom I could therefore not accept. I suppose I was a bit slow in the uptake, but I knew no one named Anne, and 'the Lady Anne' never entered my head. Then, as you will see from the second extract, she made another attempt at the end of the sitting, and made herself known to me. I am checking up with the Canon (P.-W.) about the reference to her hand.

It is all the more remarkable because such a thing never entered my head, so she could not have been in my mind at all. I naturally only expected some contact with my own relatives.

I felt that I must hasten to send these notes along to you, which I took down verbatim.

Yours,
(Reg.)

P.S. This seems to corroborate the truth of all the Canon's sittings through the years!

Extracts from a private sitting with Mrs Jean Thompson on Saturday morning, 25th February, 1956.

At the beginning of the sitting my wife Marjorie and my mother came through with some considerable evidential items, and then the guide, Sister Margaret, said :

Sister M. 'Your mother and Marjorie are now standing aside for another lady. This lady is Anne.'

Self. 'I am sorry. I do not know an Anne in spirit. I know an Anne on earth.'

Sister M. 'No. This Anne is in spirit. She has quite definitely come here for you.'

Self. 'Well, I'm sorry, but I do not know her at all. But I will make a note of her name, and see if I can trace her in any way later.'

Sister M. 'Very well. Then I will let your mother come back.'

Right at the end of the sitting, 40 minutes later—

Sister M. 'Marjorie is standing aside again for the lady who came to you a little earlier. The lady named Anne.'

Self. 'I'm very sorry, but I do not know any Anne in spirit.'

Sister M. 'She has come on to your vibration for a particular purpose. She is no relative. You have never known her. Just a minute. Wait. She is not of a recent passing. Oh, this is strange. She takes me back over centuries ! She says you may know her as "the Lady Anne".'

Self. (In amazement.) 'This is remarkable ! I had never thought of her ! Of course I know now. I am so sorry I could not accept her when she came earlier, but I never thought of her coming to me.'

Sister M. 'She says you have a great bearing on her life in connection with future events. Her life was a great tragedy. I see her in what looks like a big castle. Oh – (in surprised tone) – she is to do with Royalty ! There is another lady connected with her life – a Lady Grey. She has been impressing her thoughts on another gentleman friend of yours. There were very dark pictures in her life. Oh, she now gives me the period. She takes me back to the Tudor days. Oh – (again surprised tone) – she is one of Henry's queens ! She is – Anne Boleyn !'

Self. 'I am very privileged that she should have come through to me today. Would you ask her if she has some special message she wishes to give me.

Sister M. 'Yes. She says her story MUST be published. She wishes to add a piece of evidence – about one of her hands. Six fingers she says.'

Self. 'I'm afraid I know nothing about that, but I will ask my clergyman friend.'

Sister M. 'She wishes you to help him with her story.'

Self. 'Well, it is all written and completed. Would you ask her in what way I can help him.'

Sister M. (Rather long pause.) (Then in faint voice.) 'I'm afraid I must go. My instrument is coming back. Good day.'

APPENDIX II

(Communications purporting to be from the late Canon Pakenham-Walsh since his passing)

Sitting with sensitive (name not known) taken anonymously (by Mrs G. Vivian) at 33 Belgrave Square. 28.7.60.

A clergyman is here now, making a very great effort to get through to you—he has such a very kind face—white hair—and has not been over here very long—he thinks about 12 weeks. (P.W. died April 25th, 1960.) He is very excited to come to you today and says 'I am expected and you have sent thoughts to me to come. Much as I knew about things on earth, it is very bewildering here still'. He now writes C P W, does this convey to you who he is?

G.V. P.W. yes–but not C— oh yes I can place C (C anon P akenham-W alsh) (this was not said aloud but thought).

M. He laughs and says you knew he would get through to you, and adds 'I am more than glad I am here. I searched for truth on earth, but here it is indeed beyond all I thought. I'm glad that review (*Empire News*) was reasonably fair; I endeavoured to help the man who wrote it, for it was all true what I put in my book (*Tudor Story*) though I've not had any contact with Lady Anne yet'.

G.V. Is she your affinity, as you told me on earth?

M. P.W. is smiling and says 'I don't know yet, but all received, with overwhelming evidence, on earth *is* quite correct. I am afraid as P-H (Pearce-Higgins) said "fantastic" but no one can doubt repeated confirmation through different sensitives. He adds that he knows how you miss him. He has such a kind face, and used to live in a vicarage. I shall slip in soon and watch you all (*i.e.* at C.F.P.S. Council meetings when I've gathered the necessary experience – this is just to give you evidence that it is me speaking. . . . I will come with Joyce (G.V.'s dead daughter) to fetch you when your time comes. Maurice Elliott (former C.F.P.S. secretary) is here and says he is so glad his colleague P.W. got through to you his identity. He puts his arm through the Canon's, and says he gave you his initials straight away, no preamble, and will you pass this on as evidence to everyone you can. He *is* a lovely soul – there are no discords in this communication with you today, for you waited just the right time before trying to contact him (*i.e.* about 3 months after passing). He used to speak to people in the spirit life when he was on earth, but he is *so* glad to *be in* the spirit life'. He says 'I've been storing up power for this sitting'. Maurice says 'This sitting has been very good, I didn't always trust "trance" but I have come to bear witness to this sitting today'. P.W. says 'God bless you I give you my love and shall always be returning to you, for you collaborated with me and wrote for me on earth'.

G.V.   'Can you tell me where that shortened MSS. is we did to-gether of your book – it can't be found.' (P-H had reported to Mrs Vivian that Mrs Stubbs – the Canon's daughter could not find the MSS. of the *Tudor Story*.)

M.   'I will lead my daughter to it mentally as I don't want her to take a sitting yet – it is in his house where he lived with his daughter.' (Correct. N.B. His daughter found it the same day, and P-H rang G.V. up next morning to say that it had arrived. P-H did not know that G.V. had taken this sitting.)

———————

2nd sitting on 4.5.62, with Mrs Bess Hewitson (Mrs Vivian).

There is a gentleman here now who has a link with you – a book – a clergyman. There is also here a lady with crown – this links with the book. The gentleman is laughing and says 'I did receive the right communications for my book – Anne is here'. The gentleman is plac-ing a crown on her and says 'This is a verification and to show you I was not fooled. I am Anne's affinity and I had communication while on earth with this lady. Pearce-Higgins has received this book kindly, and has worked hard for the truth of this book. He says he has met Harry or Henry, and he is now making good progress. He says he knows how pleased you will be to have the verification of what he told you on earth (I was not fooled)'.